BASIC ILLUSTRATED

Winter Hiking and Camping

Molly Absolon

D1508500

FALCONGUIDES

GUILFORD, CONNECTICUT
HELENA, MONTANA

AN IMPRINT OF GLOBE PEQUOT PRESS

FALCONGUIDES®

FalconGuides is an imprint of Globe Pequot Press.
Falcon, FalconGuides, and Outfit Your Mind are registered trademarks of Morris Book Publishing, LLC.

Additional photo credits: pp. iv, x by Molly Absolon; p. 112 by Allen O'Bannon
Text design: Karen Williams [intudesign.net]
Project editor: Julie Marsh
Design: Karen Williams (intudesign.net)
Layout: Sue Murray

Library of Congress Cataloging-in-Publication Data

Absolon, Molly.
 Basic illustrated winter hiking and camping / Molly Absolon.
     p. cm.
 Summary: "Richly photographed and information-packed tools for the novice or handy reference for the veteran, BASIC ILLUSTRATED books distill years of knowledge into affordable and visual guides. Whether you're planning a trip or thumbing for facts in the field, the BASIC ILLUSTRATED series shows you what you need to know. BASIC ILLUSTRATED Winter Hiking and Camping Discover how to: Prepare for your trip Choose proper equipment Select safe and warm clothing Make snow shelters and set up tents on snow Cook delicious winter cuisine Stay safe in the snowy backcountry Make a winter camping repair kit" — Provided by publisher.
 ISBN 978-0-7627-7866-9 (pbk.)
 1. Snow camping. 2. Snow camping—Equipment and supplies. 3. Hiking. 4. Hiking—Equipment and supplies. I. Title.
 GV198.9.A27 2012
 796.54—dc23
                                                                            2012017912

Printed in the United States of America
10 9 8 7 6 5 4 3 2 1

Contents

Introduction   *v*

Chapter 1: Before You Go   *1*

Chapter 2: Winter Travel Equipment and Techniques   *13*

Chapter 3: Winter Clothing and Gear   *43*

Chapter 4: Living in the Snow   *65*

Chapter 5: Winter Cuisine   *85*

Chapter 6: Winter Hazards   *93*

Chapter 7: A Final Word   *109*

Appendix   *110*

    Repair Kit Checklist   *110*

    Day Pack Checklist   *111*

Index   *113*

About the Author   *118*

Introduction

I did not begin winter hiking and camping the way I recommend you begin. My first experience was a nine-day trip in western Wyoming in January 1991. It was an instructor-training course, so we were worked hard. Plus there was a glitch in our rations, and we ran short of food. Most of my memories are of being hungry, shoveling snow, struggling to pull a sled up hills and then avoid being knocked over by it on the way down, more shoveling, and generally being miserable. But there were moments even then when I caught a glimpse of why you might want to go.

A few more trips, a few more tricks, and a few more years later, winter has become one of my favorite times to be in the outdoors.

Winter is a beautiful, magical time to explore. JERAMIE PRINE

Rime-coated trees glow in the early morning light. ALLEN O'BANNON

Once I figured out how to stay comfortable in the cold and snow, I found myself enjoying the environment and seeing the beauty. And it is beautiful.

They say the Inuits have a hundred words for snow (they also say that is not true, but I still like the idea). That won't surprise anyone who has spent time out in the winter. Snow transforms the world in so many ways, you need an expanded vocabulary to explain it. Flat feathery crystals of surface hoar form like dew during clear nights, leaving behind glittering fields of diamonds that hiss as you ski through them. Rime frost coats everything, transforming trees into ghostly forests and blades of grass into shards of glass. Powdery snow piles up into rounded mounds, softening nature's hard edges and muting its palette.

Besides the beauty of the winter environment, the physical and mental challenge it provides is incredibly rewarding. You have to work to take care of yourself. You can't just fill your water bottle in

Snow allows you to play, build, and have fun outdoors. MOLLY ABSOLON

a stream; rather, you need to start your stove to melt snow to drink. You can't leave your boots out overnight, or you'll have frozen blocks to put on in the morning. If you drop a mitten on the ground, it can disappear under the snow. And even walking often means wallowing, sweating, and groveling through deep powder.

That said, the opposite is also true of winter. It is the one environment in which you can truly play. Snow is malleable, so you can build things: forts, houses, kitchens, toboggan runs, jumps, sculptures. You can roll around in it, wrestling with friends to get

Getting out in the winter can begin with building a snow fort in your backyard.
MOLLY ABSOLON

warm. You can fall back and land with a plop, snow spraying up around you as you wave your arms and legs to create a snow angel. And you can slide down it, on skis, on a sled, on your feet.

So what does it mean to go out in the winter? It can mean just about anything really. It can mean building a snow shelter in your yard after the first big dump. It can mean hiking up a well-worn path for an hour or two. It can mean cross-country skiing on a snowmobile trail. It can mean skinning up a peak to ski back down. It can mean loading up and heading out for an overnight trip into the wilderness. These are all ways to get outside, feel the bite of the cold on your cheeks, see the transformed landscape, bond with friends, and have some fun.

And your first experience doesn't have to be like mine. In fact, I encourage you to avoid such a deep initial immersion into winter recreation, as it is likely to turn you off forever. I might have avoided going out in the cold again after that trip if it hadn't been for the fact that, having just been trained as an instructor, I had a winter course to work two weeks after my return to civilization. On that course I realized you don't have to be hungry if you bring enough food, and food goes a long way in helping to keep you happy. I also learned that every day doesn't have to be a death march. You can make short moves or no moves. You can base camp and go day touring. You can even go back to your house to sleep after a long day outside.

This book is designed to help you catch the winter bug without too many bumps along the way. You'll find tips on how to choose a destination, what kind of gear you need, travel and camping techniques, and a section on backcountry hazards. Ultimately, no book can replace experience, but as my friend Buck Tilton once wrote, "Experience is a good teacher, but it also can be cruel, heartless and, in some cases, deadly."

So read this book, gather information, find a mentor, and then choose your partners and destinations with care. Be conservative in the beginning and up the challenge slowly as you gain competence. Consider taking a course or seeking out more experienced friends to guide you. Remember, the point is not to suffer unduly, but to have fun.

CHAPTER 1

Before You Go

Choosing Your Mode of Transportation

You have a few options for getting around in the winter: Your feet, snowshoes, and skis or a snowboard are the main ones if you choose to avoid engines. Each of these methods has pros and cons. I am a fan of backcountry downhill skis myself, but that's because I live in a place where it's easy to find skiable slopes within a mile or less of the car. In other places snowshoes or boots would probably be a more efficient and more enjoyable way to get around.

In making your choice, consider the places you want to go and the type of snow you expect to encounter. With this information in mind, let's look more closely at your options.

Your Feet

Hiking Boots

The easiest, least gear-intensive way to travel in the winter is to simply walk in your hiking boots. You don't need much in the way of equipment, although a nice pair of warm waterproof boots and a pair of gaiters to keep the snow out of your socks will make you more comfortable. You also don't require extensive training. If you can walk—well, you can walk.

When the snow is deep, walking without snowshoes or skis can involve arduous postholing. MOLLY ABSOLON

In much of the country, however, hiking in the winter can be difficult. Why? Because even if you have size 15 feet, they are still tiny compared to your weight, and when you step onto soft, glittery powder, your foot is going to punch down to the ground. This is called *postholing* because it's akin to stepping into a posthole—deep, awkward, and potentially dangerous if you land wrong or hit something hidden underneath.

But it's not always like that. A couple of inches of snow is easy to walk through, and the only real problem it may cause you is wet

In many popular areas, such as the Old Faithful geyser basin in Yellowstone National Park, trails get beaten down by use, allowing you to hike without snowshoes or skis on a work-hardened surface that supports your weight. MOLLY ABSOLON

boots and cold feet. To prevent that, you can wear overboots, such as those made by Neos, to keep the snow out and your feet dry.

In some places people establish a beaten-down path along popular routes, so you can hike without special equipment. The first person to put in the track has to work really hard, but if you follow behind, it can be as easy as climbing a ladder or walking down a sidewalk and is a great way to get outdoors in the winter without a lot of gear or training.

Snowshoes

When humans first moved into snowy climes, they were forced to figure out some way to move over the top of snow. It was either that or die, to be blunt. Postholing expended way too much energy for people struggling to survive. So early humans learned from the animals around them and made themselves big feet, or snowshoes, to move about in the winter.

Snowshoeing isn't really much different from hiking. You don't need a lot of skill development to be able to walk in snowshoes. If you can walk with reasonable ease, you can snowshoe. Snowshoes keep you on top of the snow (at least in most conditions), thereby allowing you the freedom to leave the beaten path to venture off on your own.

With snowshoes you can enjoy your favorite haunts even when snow makes hiking difficult. JERAMIE PRINE

Skis

Skis allow you to glide across the snow—although maybe the word *glide* is a bit of an overstatement for some of the skiing I've done. Conditions and terrain can make skiing as much of a slog as any form of winter transportation. But there's no denying that when you turn around and go downhill, you'll beat anyone on snowshoes or foot. And skiing can be a lot of fun. There's nothing like deep powder, glittering snow, and the wide-open empty spaces of winter to give you a sense of freedom and joy. Of course, there is breakable crust . . .

The biggest downside I know to skis is that they are expensive, or can be. You can pick up cheap used skis at ski swaps or thrift stores, but if you like new gear, be prepared to put a big dent in your wallet.

Another downside to skiing is that unlike hiking or snowshoeing, it requires some skill. You can pick up the basics of cross-country skiing without too much effort, but it takes time to master its more technical aspects, such as climbing steep slopes or skiing downhill through trees. Modern equipment has made the learning curve less steep, but you'll still need to put in some effort to become proficient.

Skis are a great way to get out and explore the winter world. MOLLY ABSOLON

Snowboards

Snowboarders are not limited to lift-serviced terrain. You can either get a split board—a snowboard that divides into two "skis" for traveling—or you can use snowshoes and carry your board on your back. Either way, you too can hit the mountains and find fresh powder and untouched terrain. There's not much difference between winter hiking and camping for snowboarders than there is for snowshoers and skiers—you'll just adapt to your specific equipment.

Snowboarders, using either snowshoes or a split board for travel, can enjoy backcountry powder too. JERAMIE PRINE

And finally, skiing is more affected by snow conditions than snowshoeing is. You can have a great time walking around in snowshoes in situations where you'd be cursing if you were on skis, for example when the snow is frozen and crusty or so variable it's almost impossible to ski.

Choosing a Destination

Your skill level, fitness, and experience coupled with snow conditions and weather dictate your choice of destination. Start with a short trip, maybe just a half-day excursion or an overnight. Choose a route that is easy to follow, with minimal exposure to hazards such as avalanches, open water, or steep terrain.

Winter Hazards

We'll go into hazards in detail later in the book, but for now as you consider where you want to go, you should recognize what kind of dangers you need to avoid or minimize. In general, the biggest risks to winter travelers are cold temperatures and inclement weather, open water and dangerous ice, and avalanches.

Dealing with weather requires proper equipment and awareness. Start at home by checking the weather to ensure you are well equipped for what's expected. Once you are out, beware of changing conditions. People get in the most trouble when they try to force things. They keep hiking in a whiteout because they think the road is near or the summit close and end up lost. If you cannot see and don't have a GPS or some way to navigate, stop, hunker down, get warm, and wait. Above all, be prepared.

Frozen lakes and streams can make for easy travel, but they can also be deadly traps if the ice is not strong enough to support your weight. Before you head out look at your map to see if you need to

Winter whiteouts can make routefinding difficult. If you don't have a GPS or clear trail to follow in a storm, hunker down and wait it out. ALLEN O'BANNON

cross water. Talk to people about what you might encounter. Don't commit yourself to a route that involves crossing major bodies of water if you are not 100 percent certain the ice will be frozen thick enough to hold you. Late fall and early spring are the most hazardous times for crossing ice. Be careful.

Finally, avalanches are one of the most deadly winter hazards. Avalanches do not occur everywhere. You have to have a certain amount of snow and steep enough terrain (in general, steeper than 30 degrees, or the equivalent of a black diamond ski run) to make conditions right, but there is a risk in almost any snow-covered mountain range. Avalanches like to run on slopes that are perfect for skiing, so if you are out for turns, you need avalanche training. Even if you don't want to ski, you may be exposed to avalanches as you travel. There have been numerous avalanche fatalities in flat drainages when travelers have been caught by slides coming down from above. So, again, some avalanche awareness will be necessary for winter travelers who venture into steep mountainous terrain.

Avalanches are one of the leading causes of fatalities among winter recreationists. MOLLY ABSOLON

Trip Planning

Snow Conditions

Travel distances are determined by a number of factors, the most important of which is snow conditions. Snow comes in all sorts of shapes and textures. You may find yourself floundering through giant, sugary-faceted snow where forward progress is difficult, or you may find easy walking on a frozen-solid surface.

You can't always tell what you are going to get until you hit the trail because just a few degrees change in temperature can make a huge difference in the type of conditions you will encounter. Still, you can get a good idea by paying attention to the weather and choosing the time of year in which you venture out.

If you are relatively new to outdoor winter recreation, spring is a good time for your first excursions because the days are longer and the temperatures warmer. The snow can be wet and heavy, and you are likely to encounter sun crusts on south- and west-facing slopes, but if you are hiking or snowshoeing, that won't affect your enjoyment much.

Midwinter is the best time for powder if that is your primary lure. Usually the snowpack will be deep enough for sledding, skiing, or building shelters. But it can also be cold and stormy, so you need to be well prepared to stay comfortable.

Fall is, in my mind, the trickiest time of year. The snowpack is often thin, so hazards like stumps and rocks lurk just below the surface, where they can cause injuries. Days are

With the right equipment and some knowledge, you can stay comfortable and happy in extreme conditions.
ALLEN O'BANNON

short, so you spend an awful lot of time in your tent. Still, fall has its own unique appeal. The world is in transition, animals are moving, and very few people are out there.

Terrain

I choose my winter destinations based on the skiing potential of the area, but you may be after a completely different experience. Forests are transformed by winter, making them magical places to explore, and the travel is often relatively easy, with a blanket of snow covering deadfall and other obstacles. If you are on foot, look for open, windswept, or south-facing slopes where snow levels will be minimal, making travel easier.

Snowshoes work best on flat or gradual slopes. Steep terrain is doable, especially in mountaineering-style snowshoes that have an aggressive cleat underfoot, but it can be tricky. Side-hilling is also challenging, so if you are new to the sport, look for rolling, open terrain for your early snowshoe adventures.

Some people look for good ski terrain on their winter tours; others want scenery, mountain summits, hot springs, wildlife, or any number of other objectives.
ALLEN O'BANNON

When the snow is deep, trail breaking can be hard work. It helps to take turns out in front. ALLEN O'BANNON

Distances

Travel distances can be hard to pinpoint because of the wide range of variables you have to take into consideration. In the summer most of us average 2 to 4 miles per hour in the backcountry. The low end of the range is typical for off-trail, hilly travel; the upper end for flat, even trails. You probably have a sense of your own travel speed if you hike a lot. But winter is different.

If you expect to break trail, halve the distance you would go on a summer hiking trip. If you are on a well-broken trail—on skis, snowshoes, or foot—your pace will be closer to your summer pace, *but* things will still take longer. You have to add and subtract layers of clothing all the time, you need to eat more, and you've got more stuff. So, even if your travel pace is close to your normal summer-hiking pace, I still recommend starting off with a short excursion.

In summer you typically add the equivalent of 1 mile's travel time for every 1,000 feet of elevation gain. This formula works for the winter as well. But for downhill travel, things change, especially if you are on skis. Again, skill level and snow conditions affect your speed, but you can descend 1,000 feet in minutes on skis. So, typically, when I am considering travel times and distances, I do not bother to factor in the time it takes me to ski down a slope. Instead, I assess the linear travel distance and the elevation gained to come up with my estimated travel time.

Unless I am cross-country skiing on a groomed trail, I expect to travel less than 5 to 8 miles on a good full day out in the winter. More commonly I travel 4 miles or less, especially if I am fully loaded down with camping gear. I may cover more miles than this going up and down—or yo-yoing—a slope to ski, but my travel distance car-to-car is going to be relatively modest for most day trips.

To start off, climb a peak you've done before, hike a trail that gets a fair bit of traffic, go with a knowledgeable friend, and choose a modest distance. Keep track of how long it takes you to get a sense of your individual travel speed. Make note of

It takes minutes to descend a slope that can take hours to climb in the winter.
ALLEN O'BANNON

Whether you are boot packing, skinning, or snowshoeing, uphill travel through deep snow is slow and arduous. JERAMIE PRINE

conditions so you can factor that variable in. This will help you choose destinations in the future.

If you are really a rookie, look into outdoor clubs or groups in your area that host classes on winter hiking and camping or sponsor hikes where you can meet people with similar interests. The Appalachian Mountain Club offers a variety of options for people in the Northeast. Out West, you can hook up with the Sierra Club or the Mountaineers. Or if you have the time and inclination, the National Outdoor Leadership School (NOLS) offers stellar winter programs. I know that is a shameless promotional plug, but I don't work at the school anymore and get no kickbacks for pushing their programs—I just know they do a great job of introducing people to the winter environment.

CHAPTER 2

Winter Travel Equipment and Techniques

Once you've decided what form of transportation you intend to use, you need to narrow your options one step further. Snowshoes and skis come in all kinds of shapes and sizes and are designed for a variety of different activities and body types. There are models for women and for racing. There are inexpensive, multipurpose styles and pricey, specialized varieties. In this chapter we'll look more closely at what is out there to help guide your decision.

Snowshoes

The precise origin of snowshoes is not known, but there is evidence of snowshoes dating back at least 8,000 years and probably longer. Modern snowshoes come in a variety of models designed for different activities and ranging in price from less than $100 to more than $300. All come with a rotating binding that allows you to flex your foot for more comfortable, natural walking.

Trailspace Backcountry Gear Guide (www.trailspace.com/articles/snowshoes.html) is a great place to go for information on snowshoes. You'll find articles about snowshoe selection and links to different brands so you can compare prices and models and read reviews.

What Type of Snowshoe Suits You?

To determine the type of snowshoe best suited for your purposes, use the following questionnaire:

(1) You prefer packed trails and rolling terrain. If **yes** go to (2); if **no** go to (5).

(2) You want to run or race. If **yes** go to (3); if **no** go to (4).

(3) Running or racing snowshoes are the best bet for you. These snowshoes tend to be smaller and lighter, so you can run with a natural stride over packed or groomed trails. They do not have a lot of flotation, however, so if you venture off firm snow, you are likely to sink down. Often these snowshoes have a fixed binding, which means the tail is attached to the binding with an elastic strap that keeps it from dragging. A fixed binding is great for running, but less ideal for climbing where you want more ankle flex.

(4) Recreational snowshoes are best for beginners and casual users. They tend to be the least expensive option available, so materials may not be quite as durable as more expensive models, and the binding is less aggressive, making them less suited for steep terrain. These snowshoes are also on the smaller side because they are not designed for people carrying a lot of heavy camping gear. Recreational snowshoes are ideal for easy to moderate terrain and for hiking on packed or groomed trails.

(5) You want to get off trail and be able to climb up steeper terrain, but your main goal is winter day-hiking. If **yes** go to (6); if **no** go to (7).

(6) Hiking snowshoes are more rugged and durable than recreational models. They are better suited for off-trail travel and equipped with cleats to allow you to kick your way up steeper slopes. These snowshoes are suitable for the majority of winter hiking use. They may or may not have a climbing bar attached to the binding to support your heel when ascending steep slopes.

(7) Backcountry or mountaineering snowshoes are designed to tackle steep terrain. They offer the most flotation underfoot to accommodate the combined weight of a person with gear. They have the most aggressive binding, with a climbing bar under your heel to use on steep ascents. The cleats on mountaineering snowshoes have prongs to bite into firm snow, and the bindings are made to accommodate bigger boots (snowboard or mountaineering boots). These snowshoes are made

Snowshoes come in all shapes and sizes depending on where you want to go, what you want to do, and how much you weigh. MOLLY ABSOLON

from strong materials for enhanced durability. They are the toughest and beefiest on the market, but for many of us, they are total overkill. Think about what you plan to do, talk to an expert, and buy accordingly. You don't need to have these snowshoes for a stroll in the park.

More Considerations

You'll need to know a few other things to help you determine the appropriate snowshoe for your needs.

a. What do you weigh, and how much gear do you intend to carry? The heavier that combined weight is, the bigger the snowshoe you will need.

b. What kind of snow conditions do you expect to encounter? Dry, powdery snow requires a bigger snowshoe than firm, wet snow.

Most snowshoes are held in place by a series of straps around your foot, so it's important your boot is stiff enough to withstand the force. JERAMIE PRINE

Accessories

Boots

For most snowshoeing, you will want to wear hiking boots. Look for boots with good support for your ankles and with enough structural integrity to allow you to tighten the bindings of the snowshoe without collapsing the boot. Insulated boots or boots that are roomy enough to allow you to wear two pairs of socks will help keep your feet warm. You may be able to wear pack boots with your snowshoes, but I find them to be too sloppy for most hiking. Pack boots are nice and warm, however. Some snowshoes are designed to be worn with mountaineering boots, so the bindings are extra roomy.

Ski or Trekking Poles

If you are just planning to walk around the golf course or up an easy path, you won't need poles. But once you get off into powdery snow, poles can help with balance, impulsion, and support. A regular pair of ski poles will suffice, although trekking poles have the advantage of being adjustable so you can lengthen and shorten them for going uphill and going downhill. Most of the baskets on trekking poles will be too small for snow, so you'll want to trade them out for a bigger basket that won't plunge down all the way to the ground on each step.

Travel Techniques

Walking over Flats

For the most part, walking with snowshoes is the same as walking without. You may find that you walk with your feet slightly wider apart than normal so you don't trip over the snowshoes, but in general, strive to have an easy, natural gait. In soft snow exaggerate the lift of your knees to clear the snow with your snowshoe.

Walking Uphill

You will be most comfortable walking straight up a hill in snowshoes instead of switching back and forth across the slope. Snowshoes are designed to let you kick your toes into the snow, forming a step as you move uphill. Your foot will rotate forward in the binding, allowing your toes to drop below the snowshoe deck so you can kick into the snow. The cleat below the ball of your foot gives you additional purchase as you kick steps upward. Try not to lean too far forward, or you may find yourself slipping. Rather, stay upright, with your weight centered over the ball of your foot.

If you do decide to traverse a slope, stomp down with your foot, creating a platform with each step. In soft snow you'll find you can create a level trail for your feet with this technique. If the snow is too firm, side-hilling becomes increasingly difficult.

Walking in snowshoes doesn't require any special technique. Just walk with your normal stride. JERAMIE PRINE

Walking Downhill

Again, because of the geometry of the snowshoe, you are better off heading straight down a slope rather than trying to traverse it. Face downhill and bend at your hips so your nose is over your toes, as we like to say. This position keeps your weight centered over your feet. If you lean too far back, you're likely to slip and fall onto your butt.

Step forward, kicking down into the snow with your heel. Be aggressive with each kick so your heel sinks in and gives you a good, solid platform to stand on. You can kick your way downhill quite rapidly using this technique.

Turns

For the most part, just walk around a turn, taking care not to step on the inside of your opposite snowshoe. In tight areas you may find that you need to do a kick turn, where you lift up one knee and turn your foot away from you so the toes on that foot are facing the opposite direction of the toes on your other foot, heels together. This is ballet's fifth position, for those of you who understand that term. Step onto the forward foot and swing your back leg around so both feet are facing in the same direction.

You may want to practice this turn a few times on level ground to make sure you have it. The technique is not hard, but it can be awkward, especially on a hillside or in tight quarters.

Walking Backward

Occasionally you may have to back up on your snowshoes. Because the tail of the snowshoe drags along behind, it can be a bit awkward to take a step in reverse. The trick is to lift your knee high, so the tail is hanging above the snow, then move your foot back, step, and repeat.

Breaking Trail

In soft snow the person out front is going to have to work harder than those following behind. Breaking trail requires more energy because your foot sinks down with each step, so you have to lift it up to clear the snow as you move ahead.

To conserve energy, your best bet is to take turns being out front. Those following behind can step into the leader's footprints and have an easier go of it. You can also step half in, half out of the track, creating a larger footprint with each step. Using this technique, you'll find you end up with a continuously beaten-down walking path, which will be easier for people following behind, as there isn't a wall of snow for them to clear with each step.

Falling and Getting Up

It's not uncommon for people to trip themselves up when they first start walking on snowshoes. Fortunately, you usually don't have a lot of momentum, so a fall on snowshoes is more awkward and embarrassing than dangerous. If you find yourself falling, try not to stick out a hand or pole to save yourself, as that can cause you to dislocate a shoulder or injure your wrist. Your best bet is to plop down on your butt, but barring that, try to tuck your shoulder down—almost as if you were going to roll over—and take the brunt of your fall on your upper back. Hopefully, you'll just land in a puff of powder.

Getting up in powder can be tricky. You go to push down with your hand and your arm plunges into the snow, causing you to face-plant. If you are using ski poles, take the poles and make a cross in the snow. Put one hand in the center of the cross and push off of it as you stand up. I like to push myself forward onto my knees before standing up, as it takes less energy.

If you are wearing a heavy pack, take it off before trying to rise. It's just too awkward and strenuous to try to get up in soft powder with those extra pounds on your back.

Skis

Like snowshoes, skis come in a wide range of styles and shapes. The type you end up using will depend on your specific goals.

You can spend a lot of money on ski equipment, so if you are new to the sport, do some research and rent equipment until you figure out what gear is best suited to your skill level and goals. Magazines like

Single- versus Double-camber Skis

In general, skis come with either single or double camber. Camber is the bend in the ski underfoot. With Nordic (cross-country) skis, you will see a distinct bow shape in the middle of the skis, such that when you hold two skis together base to base, they touch at the tip and tails but have space under the binding area. This space is a result of the skis' camber.

Nordic skis typically have double camber, making them hard to flatten. The bow is your wax pocket, or where your fish scales will be on waxless skis. The idea is that when you weight that part of the ski by stepping down onto it, you flatten out the bow and the wax or scales come into contact with the snow, allowing you to kick off and push yourself forward. When you unweight the ski, the bow curves up, the sticky wax leaves the snow, and you glide forward. These skis are designed to allow you to kick and glide and are primarily for touring in rolling or flat terrain.

If you are out to make alpine turns, you'll want a single-camber ski. When you take single-camber skis and hold them base to base, there is very little curve and they press together easily. Single-camber skis do not glide as well on the flats as double-camber skis because you don't get much lift off the snow, but they are better for turning because the edge stays in contact with the snow throughout the turn.

Single-camber downhill skis versus double-camber Nordic touring skis.

MOLLY ABSOLON

Backcountry, Cross Country Skier, Powder, and *Ski* do annual gear reviews, and you can search online for forums that debate the latest and greatest equipment. Or go to a trustworthy backcountry ski shop and ask advice. Tell the salesperson exactly what you hope to do, how much you can spend, and what type of skier you are, and he or she should be able to guide you to the appropriate ski.

What Type of Ski Is for You?

Deciding if you want single- or double-camber skis is just the first step in narrowing down your options. Ask yourself the following questions to help you home in on the right style for you.

(1) You primarily want to ski through woods and meadows over rolling terrain. If **yes** go to (2); if **no** go to (5).

(2) You prefer groomed trails. If **yes** go to (3); if **no** go to (4).

(3) If you plan to focus on groomed Nordic ski trails, you should look for a lightweight, classic cross-country ski with double camber or a skate ski.

(4) If you prefer ungroomed trails or off-trail travel but are still primarily focused on touring rather than downhill skiing, you should look for a double-camber touring ski, which will be slightly heavier and wider than a lightweight classic ski.

(5) If you are looking to explore rugged, ungroomed terrain but skis are primarily a form of transportation, go to (6). If you are mainly interested in making alpine turns, go to (7).

Ski tourers can choose between a lightweight Nordic ski, best suited for groomed trails, and a slightly wider touring ski, best suited for venturing off into untracked snow. MOLLY ABSOLON

(6) For traveling off trail in difficult terrain, you should look into a pair of metal-edged, double-camber waxless skis. Metal edges will make your skis heavier and a bit more cumbersome when kicking and gliding, but the edges will give you better control skiing through trees or on tight, twisting descents around obstacles.

(7) If your priority is to make turns and your travel is aimed solely at gaining access to downhill terrain, you should look into a pair of metal-edged telemark or alpine-touring (AT) skis. How do you decide between telemark and AT skis? Both are great options. I used to be a tele-skier, but then I switched to AT. Telemark turns are gorgeous, challenging, fun, and more work (at least for me). Tele-gear also used to be lighter than AT gear, but these days that is no longer the case. Some AT bindings are superlight, and some are pretty beefy. Your goals will determine

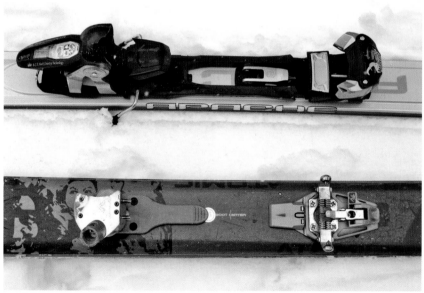

Heavy AT bindings (top) are better suited for "sidecountry" skiing where you want lots of support and don't plan to tour for long distances, while lightweight Dynafit bindings (bottom) are ideal for backcountry skiing. MOLLY ABSOLON

which type is best suited for your needs. If you plan to use your skis at a resort more often than in the backcountry, you're probably better off with the heavier bindings. Also, if you ski steep, aggressive terrain, you may find the beefier bindings are better. Lightweight bindings are great if you plan to do lots of backcountry touring.

Wax versus Waxless

If you are using a touring ski (as opposed to a downhill ski), you will need to decide whether you want to use wax or not. Waxless skis have plastic fish scales or ridges below your foot to grip into the snow, preventing you from sliding backward. Kick wax provides the same function for waxable skis.

Waxless skis are the easiest to use and have excellent grip in every condition except ice or very firm snow, so they adapt well to changing snow conditions. Waxless skis tend to be a bit slower than waxable skis, but they aren't nearly as clunky and slow as they were ten years ago. Waxable skis are higher performing than waxless when you get the wax right for the type of snow you encounter, but are horrible when you get it wrong; therefore, they can be difficult in variable conditions. Waxable skis are best when you expect conditions to remain constant and you are looking to optimize speed. High-end racers typically use waxed skis because they are faster, but if snow conditions are funky, they may opt for waxless.

For most recreational Nordic skiers, waxless skis, which have fish scales on the base to provide traction, are the most versatile and forgiving.
MOLLY ABSOLON

Wax

There are two categories of ski wax: glide wax and kick wax. Glide wax is the kind you coat your base with to maximize your ability to slide across the snow. It is applied with a hot iron to ensure penetration into the base of your skis, and the excess is scraped off. Most ski shops will wax your skis relatively cheaply, or you can do it at home with an old iron and a plastic scraper. Glide wax is used on both Nordic and downhill skis to create a frictionless surface on the bottom of your skis. If your friends are losing you on the out-track, you probably need to rewax your skis.

Kick wax is the opposite of glide wax: It is designed to provide friction or grip so you can push your way forward with each step. Without kick wax, you'd just slide backward. Kick wax comes in little color-coded metal canisters. You rub it on the bottom of your ski in the so-called wax pocket that lies beneath your foot.

There are probably thirty types of kick wax, each blended to work in different snow temperatures. Warmer colors—reds and purples—are used for softer waxes that hold best on warmer snow. Cooler colors—greens and blues—are used for hard waxes that are designed to be used with cold snow.

If you do end up with waxable skis, you should probably get some instruction on waxing. For most of my backcountry skiing, I tend to slap skins onto my skis when I'm on the flats or climbing. That said, I do use wax sometimes when I have a long approach over rolling terrain, and I have picked up some tricks over the years for this kind of combat waxing. If you are a classic Nordic skier, you'll understandably scoff at these tricks—they are way too general and unrefined for the sophisticated Nordic skier—but they work for backcountry.

Rule number 1: If you are on single-camber, heavy downhill skis, you'll want a big wax pocket and lots of wax—nothing like the little 15-inch pocket underfoot you typically use on a lightweight Nordic ski. Instead, go big and go thick. The wax will wear off quickly with your flat, clunky skis, plus you need a lot more stick with heavier gear.

Rule number 2: Don't overthink it. Waxing can be a science project or it can be pretty basic. If you are on big clunky skis, you aren't going to be finessing things. Err on the cold side when choosing your wax, as you can always add a warmer one on top. But remember the old peanut butter and jelly analogy: You can't spread peanut butter on jelly. Warm waxes are like jelly; cold waxes are harder and won't stick to them, so it's best to start hard and move toward soft as needed.

For a rough estimate of snow temperature, make a snowball. Perfect snowball snow usually calls for extra blue or special purple wax—something in the middle of the range. Snowballs that leave your hands wet require a warmer wax, purple up into red. If the snow is dry and cold, it won't stick together into a snowball. In this situation you'll be using a blue down into green-colored wax.

To further complicate things, each wax color comes with an "extra" and "special" version. These colors cover the in-between areas, sort of like the halfway mark. At NOLS we used the expression "extra stick, special glide" to help us remember the difference: Extra was on the warmer end of a color when you needed a little extra stick, while special was on the colder end when you wanted more glide. I only bring this up because I've found that in the Rocky Mountains with single-camber skis, I almost always use either extra blue or special purple wax regardless of the ambient air temperature. I'm not sure why, but those colors seem to be the most versatile for a hack waxer like me.

So glop the wax on nice and thick under your foot. If you are on flat, single-camber skis, make that pocket big—2 feet or longer. Once the wax is on, you can take a cork and smooth it out. Corking creates a more even covering and will give you higher performance, especially if you are on lightweight classic gear. If you are on heavy stuff, it's probably not worth corking.

Finally, there is klister. I have to admit I have never used klister and have only heard horror stories about it. Klister is designed for old or warm snow that other waxes don't grip. It usually comes in a tube and is very sticky and messy, but if you find yourself in conditions where nothing else works, klister is a lifesaver. Some people recommend covering the bottom of your skis with duct tape and applying klister onto the tape. Then when you are done, you just rip off the tape. Otherwise, you have a sticky mess on the bottom of your skis that can be difficult to remove.

How Long?

The length of your ski will vary according to its function and width. If you are a beginner, you'll be looking at an alpine ski that comes up to your chin or so. Expert skiers looking to go fast are going to want something longer for added stability. Throw in the width, shape, and specialty features like the rocker, and you add more variables to determining the optimal length. If you can try out different skis, great. If not, work with a knowledgeable salesperson to match your skill and size with the best ski length.

For Nordic skis, the flex pattern and stiffness of the ski is more important than its length. If the ski is too stiff, you won't be able to get enough kick; too flexible, and you won't end up with much glide. Flex patterns affect where the ski touches the snow, again affecting glide.

Most ski manufacturers have a chart that matches your height and weight to the appropriate length ski. This is a good starting point. A trained salesperson can also help you home in on the right-size ski.

Accessories

Boots

Needless to say, your boots will be dictated by the type of skiing you are doing. In general, you want to find a boot that is warm and comfortable. Try to size the boot a bit larger than normal to allow yourself some space for two pairs of socks or at least adequate wiggle room for your toes. Rigid racing boots fitted with nylon knee socks are not going to be very comfortable or warm if you are away from the resort and its boot warmers.

Ski Poles

You may think there isn't much to consider when picking out a pair of ski poles, but you can spend up to $300 on cross-country poles, so obviously there are some things out there to be aware of.

With expensive ski poles, you are paying for light weight, stiffness, and the type of grip and basket. These factors are important to racers, but you don't necessarily need to spend

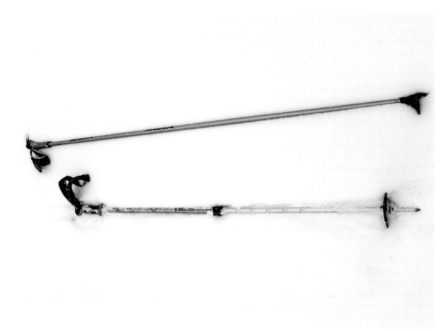

Nordic poles are long and come with small baskets and grips designed to hold your hand in place. Downhill ski poles are shorter with bigger baskets to support you in the powder. They also tend to have quick-release straps in case your pole gets caught on something as you ski. MOLLY ABSOLON

hundreds of dollars on poles for recreational purposes. Still, there are a few factors to consider when selecting your poles that don't involve lots of cash.

Some ski poles come with really wimpy baskets. These baskets work fine on hard-packed trails or at the resort, but if you get into soft powder, they plunge down deep, throwing off your balance without providing any support. If you plan to be in unpacked snow, make sure your poles have a reasonably sized basket.

The length of your pole will vary. Cross-country skiers use poles that extend above the chin or higher, while downhill skiers want a pole that allows them to bend their arm to 90 degrees when gripped below the basket on a hard floor. The longer poles are designed to give Nordic skiers extension and reach when they are cruising along. Shorter poles are used to initiate a turn while skiing downhill.

Longer poles give classic skiers extension and power. MOLLY ABSOLON

You can buy telescoping poles, or poles that can be lengthened and shortened with a simple adjustment. These poles can be used long for touring and shortened for turns.

Skins

Most downhill backcountry skiers use climbing skins rather than wax or fish scales to grip the snow. Climbing skins were originally made from animal pelts, but now most are made from synthetic materials that mimic an animal's fur. The idea is the fibers lie flat and smooth when running in one direction, but stand up on end and catch the snow in the other. Think of running your hand along your dog's back: In one direction the fur lies flat, in the other it stands up. Climbing skins do the same: As you slide forward, they glide smoothly over the snow; when you slide backward, the fibers stand up and catch to keep you from slipping.

Most climbing skins available on the market are coated with glue that sticks to the bottom of your ski. In addition, most include some

When you put your skins away, fold them together glue side in. MOLLY ABSOLON

kind of clip that attaches to the tip and tail of your ski. There are some glueless skins available that are light and involve less maintenance than glue-on skins, but the old ones—called snakeskins—were not very high performing. Newer ones that use the same synthetic fibers as glue-on skins are being developed and may become the best thing out there, but right now they are hard to find and the technology is still a bit unreliable.

To store your skins, fold them together with the glue side facing in. The skins will stick together and stay cleaner this way (too much dirt and lint in the glue affects the skin's sticking ability). Some skins work differently, but in general, to put the skins on, first pull them apart to expose the glue (with new skins, this can be hard—it may help to have someone assist you). Place the skin's tip clasp over the tip of your ski and slide your hand down the skin, pressing it onto the base, then attach the tail clasp. Repeat with the other ski, and off you go.

Try to keep the glue side of your skins out of the snow when you are putting them on or taking them off to maintain the glue's adhesive

You can remove skins without taking off your skis. (top left) First, lift the tail of your ski off the ground and remove the tail clasp. (top right) Pull forward, stripping the skin off the bottom of the ski. (bottom left) Flex your ankle so the tip of your ski comes up and continue pulling the skin forward. (bottom right) Flick the skin off the ski tip and you're done. MOLLY ABSOLON

power. Pull them off at the top of the climb and store them in your backpack or a pocket. If you are out overnight, hang your skins out to dry while you make camp. When you go to bed, bring your skins into your shelter with you. I tend to sleep with them between my sleeping bag and pad to keep them supple and help with drying.

Skin Emergency

All of us have had skin failure at one time or another. Halfway up a slope in the middle of nowhere, suddenly your skin will no longer stick. If you find yourself in this predicament, rub the glue side of the skin rapidly back and forth across your thigh. Your goal is to warm up the surface of the skin and give the glue a bit more life. Duct tape can also be used to help secure the skin to your ski if all else fails.

In wet snow conditions, skins can absorb water and ice up. You can buy commercial waterproofing wax to coat the bottom of your skins to keep the snow off, which is advisable in the spring when the snow is wet. If you find yourself faced with snow buildup without any waterproofing wax handy, scrape off the snow and ice and try applying sunscreen or rubbing candle wax over them. I've had some success with these tricks.

Take advantage of the sun during breaks or in camp to dry out your skins. Wet skins tend to freeze, causing snow buildup.

MOE WITSCHARD

To get the most out of your kick and glide, make sure you stay flexed at your ankles and extend forward with each step, taking care to transfer your weight completely from one foot to the other. MOLLY ABSOLON

Travel Techniques

Flats

When you are cruising across flat or gently rolling terrain, you want to kick and glide. On skinny Nordic skis, kicking and gliding can send you flying across the snow; on heavier equipment, it's a little faster than simply walking in your skis.

Assume an athletic stance: knees bent softly, ankles flexed, feet shoulder-width apart, shoulders slightly forward. This is your basic position. Try to hold this position throughout the movement. Now slide one foot forward, keeping your ankle flexed and your knees bent over your toes. Shift all of your weight onto that foot, pushing your other leg back and straight (this backward push is the kick).

Beginner skiers' biggest mistake is to have stiff legs. Make sure you maintain a soft bend in your knees and keep your ankles pressed forward against the tongue of your boots. MOLLY ABSOLON

Hold this pose until you feel yourself slowing down, then before you lose your forward momentum, bring your back leg forward, shift your weight onto that ski, and push with the leg that was formerly in front. In fast conditions and on the flats, you can glide in this position for a long distance.

Your arms will swing naturally in time with your legs if you let them, just like when you run. So, for example, as your left leg goes forward, your opposite (right) arm goes forward, and your left arm goes back. Bend your arm gently in front of you, planting the pole when it is beside the toe of your forward foot. You'll then push into that hand, straightening your arm as you move past the pole. This pole plant adds to your forward momentum.

Shorten your stride and increase your cadence to ski uphill. MOLLY ABSOLON

Uphill Technique

To move up gentle hills, continue to kick and glide, shortening your stride and increasing your cadence to maximize the contact of your wax or fish scales with the snow for grip.

Avoid leaning too far forward, or you will shift your weight onto your toes and cause yourself to slip backward.

To help you understand this, imagine yourself walking along a flat surface. Your feet hit the ground squarely, the entire sole making contact. Now tilt the surface so you are walking uphill. To keep your feet flat, you must flex at the ankle, right? But if you lean forward as you flex, where does the weight go? Typically it's going to focus down onto your toes, and your heels will come up. What that means is the amount of surface contact you have with the ground has shrunk from your entire foot to just the ball of your foot—not much contact, which makes it pretty easy to slip.

Your goal when ascending is to maximize the contact of your ski with the snow in order to give yourself the purchase you need to

If you lean too far forward climbing uphill, your weight shifts onto the ball of your foot, providing less contact with the snow and resulting in a tendency to slip. ALLEN O'BANNON

AT and tele-bindings come with a built-in climbing post that elevates your heel, allowing you to climb steeper terrain. This skier is using the mid-level height. ALLEN O'BANNON

Try to keep your shoulders back and weight centered over your feet when moving uphill to prevent slipping. ALLEN O'BANNON

push yourself forward. That means you want to avoid leaning too far forward. I like to think of keeping my shoulders back and pushing my hips forward when I am climbing hills. The goal is to avoid getting onto your toes and limiting the contact of your ski with the snow. **The more contact, the more purchase, and the better able you are to push yourself forward and uphill.**

Eventually the slope will get too steep for you to climb straight up. That magic angle will be determined by your technique and your equipment. Waxed and waxless skis start slipping before skis covered with climbing skins, but even skins will slip eventually. When the slope gets too steep, you have a couple of options. One is to move into a herringbone.

The herringbone is done by making a V with your skis, open side facing uphill. Roll your feet in a little at the ankles so you are on the inside edges of your skis and step up the hill, one foot after the other. This technique works great, but it's tiring and slow, and so I save it for short sections of trail.

For short sections of uphill, make a V shape with your skis, rolling your ankles in to bring the inside edges in contact with the snow, and climb up.

MOLLY ABSOLON

To sidestep, turn so your skis are perpendicular to the fall line and step one foot at a time up the hill.

MOLLY ABSOLON

Sidestepping (which is exactly what it sounds like) is a little less strenuous, but slower. Again, it's best suited for a short section of steep terrain. Sidestepping can be a little tricky when your heels are free and the tails of your skis drag. If you are using AT gear, it may be easier to lock your heels down if you need to sidestep over any distance. The key trick is to make sure your skis are perpendicular to the fall line to ensure you don't slip.

If you have to climb a big hill, you'll want to break a trail that switchbacks its way up the slope, letting you climb at a relatively low angle (6 to 10 degrees). To make a turn at the end of each traverse, either walk the corner (best on lower-angle slopes) or do a kick turn.

Fall Line

The fall line is an important concept for winter travelers. Basically it refers to the line a ball would follow as it rolls down the slope.

Kick Turn How-to

Position your skis perpendicular to the fall line. Lift your uphill ski, keeping the tip high, and arc it around until it is facing the opposite direction from the tip of your downhill ski. You will now be in fifth position, if you ever took ballet—feet parallel with heels next to the toes of the opposite foot. (It's worth practicing this move on flat terrain because it can be awkward!) Make sure you keep your skis across the fall line, or you may find yourself slipping and falling in a very awkward position.

Now step onto the ski you just moved—in this description, your uphill ski. Lift your downhill ski and step around toward the uphill until both skis are facing the same direction. Sound hard? Try it in your stocking feet right now—you'll see, it's not that complicated, although adding 6-foot planks to the bottoms of your feet does make the move a bit more challenging.

The other thing you have to figure out is what to do with your poles. In general, pole placement is a matter of practice and personal preference. Think about where your skis are going to go to avoid getting tangled up. I tend to put my poles behind my back.

Practice turning both up- and downhill to get the hang of it. In some places an uphill turn will be easiest, and if you are pulling a sled, an uphill turn is all you can do. I find downhill turns feel a bit more precarious, but there's less hillside to get in the way of your skis, so some people prefer it.

To turn in place, swing your uphill ski around until your tips face in opposite directions. Now step onto the uphill ski and swing your downhill ski around until both skis are parallel and facing in your new direction. MOLLY ABSOLON

On gentle downhills you can just let your skis run straight, but when the pitch gets steeper, you'll want to control your speed. Your technique will depend on your skis: Cross-country skiers will use a wedge, with their skis in a V shape, weighting their big toes to put pressure on the inside edges. The wider the wedge, the slower you'll go. The other way to slow yourself down is by turning, which can be hard in lightweight gear. MOLLY ABSOLON

Breaking Trail

If the snow is deep, breaking trail is arduous, so you'll want to take turns. In some conditions you may even have your trailbreakers drop their packs while out in front. They can circle back behind the group to pick up their gear after their turn is over. Following in a set track is much, much easier and faster, so those in the back usually need to wear warmer clothes and be patient with the pace until it's their turn to be out front.

When breaking trail, look ahead and plan your route. Find the easiest line: Look for low-angle slopes, gradual ridges, and forests that aren't too thick or covered with fallen trees. Try to think of rounded, arcing lines so you minimize the number of kick turns you have to do. Switch off frequently.

Falling Down and Getting Up

All skiers fall. Some fall more than others, of course, but falling is inevitable. You'll fall because you are pushing yourself and your technique, and you'll fall because you need to stop immediately and sitting down on your bum off to the side of your skis is the best way to do that quickly and with the least likelihood of injury. A controlled sit-down is the preferred falling technique, but obviously it's not always possible.

Once you are down, it can be strenuous to get up. Again, here's where the butt sit has another advantage: It's easier to get up from this position than from a full-on face-plant. Regardless, if you find yourself floundering about in deep snow, make a platform to push up on by either dropping your pack or crossing your poles into an X and pushing up where they intersect.

Make sure your skis are downhill of your body and perpendicular to the slope before you attempt to get up. You may need to roll over and untangle yourself to get into this position. If you are carrying a heavy pack or pulling a sled, take it off or let it go. You'll use less energy in the long run. As a last resort, take off your skis as well to get organized.

Falling is part of skiing, but you need to know how to get back up. ALLEN O'BANNON

It's important to learn how to get up before you fall! Getting back on your feet can be especially hard if you find yourself wallowing in soft snow The best technique is to: (top) roll yourself forward, getting your weight over your skis; (middle) make an X with your poles to give you a platform for pushing off; and (bottom) kneel forward and stand up. MOLLY ABSOLON

<blockquote>CHAPTER 3</blockquote>

Winter Clothing and Gear

Choosing Warm Clothing

Humans evolved where it was hot. We have very little hair, and our skin is laced with sweat glands designed to give off moisture to evaporate and cool us down. In some parts of the world, such as the Arctic, human residents tend to be a bit shorter and chubbier to help retain body heat, but they don't have fur or thick, blubbery fat to insulate their core like truly evolved Arctic animals. What we do have is our big brain. We can think our way to staying warm and happy in cold environments.

Animals, including humans, lose heat through convection, conduction, radiation, and evaporation. Convection is the loss of heat to water or air moving past us. Conduction is the transfer of heat through direct contact, such as by sitting on the cold ground or touching a piece of ice. Radiation is the heat we give off as a by-product of our basic metabolism. We generate heat just staying alive, and that heat is given off, or radiates—into the atmosphere. Finally, we lose heat through the evaporation of moisture— usually sweat—on our skin. A wet surface loses heat as much as twenty-five times faster than a dry one. This is great in the summer when you are hot and need to cool down, but it can be deadly in the winter.

To stay warm and comfortable in the winter, you need to fuel your internal furnace with lots of high-calorie food. ALLEN O'BANNON

The goal to staying warm and dry in the winter is to minimize heat loss and maximize its gain. Exercise ups our heat generation by as much as fifteen to eighteen times. Because of this, exercise is your best source of heat gain in the outdoors. If you feel cold, do fifty jumping jacks or go for a ski and you'll warm up.

Our other tool for dealing with the cold is to dress appropriately.

Insulation

Winter clothing is designed to insulate your body from the cold. A garment's insulating capability is dictated by its ability to trap air in enclosed spaces (dead air). Your body warms this air, and—since the air cannot move—it stays warm, thereby creating a protective layer of heat around you.

Moisture

Winter clothing must also manage moisture. As mentioned above, wet surfaces cool down much more rapidly than dry ones, so our clothing needs to protect us from rain and snow but at the same time allow moisture from our sweat to escape, or to be "breathable."

Materials

Today's outdoor clothes come with all sorts of whistles and bells. You can even buy jackets with a battery-powered heater. I've never personally used one of those, but it could be pretty nice when you are out in extreme cold. The big thing to think about is protecting yourself from the heat drains: convection, conduction, radiation, and evaporation. Thoughtful layering of different types and weights of materials will allow you to dress effectively for almost all conditions.

Synthetics

A large percentage of technical winter clothing is made from some type of synthetic material—polyester, polypropylene, nylon, or other brand-name fabrics made from petroleum-based fibers. These synthetics come in a number of different weights and can be used for everything from base layers (long underwear) to waterproof shells. Synthetics are spun into fibers that can be woven into fabrics of different thickness—the thicker the fibers, the more dead air space and the more insulation value to the garment. In addition to providing dead air space, the fibers also are designed to move, or wick, moisture away from your skin, helping it to stay relatively warm even when wet and to dry quickly.

Coated synthetics—such as you find in waterproof raingear—are used to keep moisture out, but can be too hot when you exercise. Tightly woven fabrics provide a good windbreak and some water resistance.

- **Pros:** Lightweight, maintains insulating properties when wet, relatively inexpensive, and dries quickly. Versatile and can be used for base layers, insulating layers, wind layers, and even as filling in parkas and sleeping bags.

- **Cons:** Synthetic base layers have been known to hold odors, making them rather stinky after extended wear. Synthetic filling is bulkier than down filling and can break down over time, thereby losing some of its insulating capacity.

Wool

Wool is made from spun fibers of fur, typically from sheep. Wool fibers are naturally crimped, creating dead air space for insulation. The fibers absorb moisture, allowing you to stay warm even when the fabric is wet. Wool, like synthetics, can be woven into fabrics of different weights and thickness, allowing it to be used for both base and insulating layers. If spun tightly, wool can provide some degree of windproofing, but its strength is really in its insulating capability.

Wool used to be notoriously itchy, but now you can buy finely spun merino wool that most people can wear without any discomfort. The downside to these garments is that they tend to be expensive.

- **Pros:** Maintains insulating capacity even when wet and less likely to retain odors.
- **Cons:** Can be itchy and/or expensive. Takes longer to dry than synthetics.

Down

Down is the soft under-feathers of a bird— usually a goose—that is used to fill jackets and sleeping bags. Down has incredible insulating capacity. In fact, it is so warm that you usually can't wear down when exercising, as it is too hot. Down is compressible and lightweight.

- **Pros:** Lightweight, compressible, and warm. Ideal insulating layer in cold, dry conditions.
- **Cons:** When wet, down turns into a useless rag with absolutely no insulating ability. It also takes a long time to dry; in fact, it is almost impossible to dry a soaked down garment without a dryer.

Gore-Tex

Gore-Tex was the original waterproof, breathable fabric—ideal for winter jackets and pants. The company has lost its patent on the technology behind Gore-Tex, and now there are lots of versions of the material on the market, all going under different brand names. Whichever brand name you go with, this type of material keeps you dry while still offering some breathability, making it ideal for outer layers in wintery conditions.

- **Pros:** Waterproof, breathable, and ideal for outer layers in stormy wet conditions.
- **Cons:** Can be expensive, bulky, and hot.

> Cotton has no real place out in the winter, except perhaps for a bandana to clean your sunglasses with. Cotton holds moisture and can take forever to dry, so if you sweat in cotton, you stay wet and cold.

Layering

You will find that your clothing requirements change constantly throughout the day when you are out in the winter. Climbing uphill in temperatures in the 20s may mean you are dressed only in your long underwear base layers and some wind gear, but the minute you stop, you'll need to throw on a jacket and hat. Around camp you may be dressed in multiple layers, culminating in a big insulated parka, insulated pants and booties, mittens, and a hood. And on wet, snowy

A lightweight polypropylene or wool base layer is like your second skin in winter. Add and subtract layers—like this soft-shell jacket and Gore-Tex pants— for active outdoor wear. Once you stop moving, throw on an insulated parka to keep you warm. MOLLY ABSOLON

days you may have to weigh the pros and cons of dressing to keep the snow out and sweating a bit in your nonbreathable waterproof gear, or staying cooler but getting wet in your wind gear.

Our bodies tend to shunt blood away from our extremities in cold temperatures to protect the vital organs of our core and our brains, so you need to take care to keep your hands and feet warm. Putting on or taking off a hat is an easy, quick way to regulate your temperature as you move.

Basic Winter Clothing List

Top Layers

- 2 base layers: one lightweight long underwear top that will be like your skin, one expedition-weight layer. Zip-turtlenecks are nice for at least one of these layers, as they allow you to modify the warmth of the garment by opening and closing the zipper.

- 1 or 2 insulating layers: down or synthetic jacket and possibly a pile or wool sweater, depending on expected temperatures. For overnight trips you'll definitely want two insulating layers, with one being a big winter parka.

- 1 waterproof or water-resistant storm jacket with hood

Bottom Layers

- 1 pair base-layer long underwear (your winter skin), light or medium weight depending on expected temperatures

- 1 pair storm pants (Gore-Tex or soft shell)

- For overnight trips or extremely cold day tours, bring an additional pair of insulated or shelled Capilene pants.

Feet

- 2 to 4 pairs socks. Wearing two pairs of socks gives you some extra insulation and cushioning, but if you have performance boots, you may only be able to fit in one pair. The rule of thumb is to have one pair or set of socks on your feet, and one pair or set in your pack for emergencies. On overnight trips I often bring one other pair for sleeping.

- 1 pair gaiters. Gaiters are essential to keep snow out of your boots. You'll want to make sure yours have a strap that goes

Basically, the general rule of thumb is to be ready for anything. Keep extra layers handy in your pack, and change before you find yourself too chilled or too hot.

> Having large zipper pulls on all your zippers will allow you to manipulate zippers with your mittens or gloves on. You can use parachute cord to make a zipper pull.

under your boot to keep the gaiter from riding up. Most ski pants come with built-in gaiters; these are fine if they stay down over your boots.

- For overnight trips you'll want to have some kind of bootie system that allows you to take off your boots. An insulated bootie with a sole works great. Or, if you have plastic boots with removable liners, you can pull out the liners, put in an insole, and wear insulated, sole-less booties inside the plastic shells to walk around camp. Neos makes waterproof overboots that come with a beefy sole. You can pull these overboots on over insulated booties, allowing you to walk around camp with some support and gaiters to keep you dry.

Hands

- I am a big proponent of mittens because I find them to be warmer than gloves. That said, gloves are imperative for doing any kind of work in the kitchen, on your gear, etc.
- 2 pairs lightweight gloves. For day trips it's nice to have two pairs to alternate if your hands get wet. For camping at least one pair of thin wool gloves is nice because you can handle hot things in the kitchen with wool.
- 1 pair insulated mittens or gloves

Head

- Make sure your insulated parka has a hood. Then I recommend:
- 1 wool hat
- 1 neck warmer, Buff, or balaclava

Winter Packs

When choosing a pack for winter hiking, skiing, or camping, you should consider a few things:

Ease of access: When you are wearing gloves or mittens, lots of zippers and snaps can be a pain. It's nice to have an easy way into the pack that you can access without taking off your gloves. Some packs come with a "clamshell" opening behind your back that you can unzip to get into the main body of the pack; others have a side zip that allows you access without having to open up the top. Both are nice features in the winter.

Packs that have easy access—such as this one with a zipper opening in the back—are nice in the winter. MOLLY ABSOLON

Size: Winter packs tend to need more space than summer packs simply because you are carrying bulky clothing, more food and water, a shovel, etc., so your winter daypack will be larger than your summer one.

Straps, whistles, and bells: You don't really need a lot of stuff dangling off your pack, and often these straps and things just get in the way and add weight (yes, every ounce does add up). You will probably want a way to strap skis, snowshoes, or an ice ax onto your pack, and it is nice to have a shovel pocket and perhaps a slot for an avalanche probe or the shovel handle. But otherwise, don't be sold on too many external doodads—they add weight and most of the time go unused.

Materials: Nowadays packs are made of lighter and lighter materials. This is great for the winter, since you already are forced to bring more stuff for safety's sake. You don't need a fully waterproof pack in most conditions in the winter, since water is frozen, but if you are in a place with lots of wet snow, you may opt for waterproof materials or just line your pack with a plastic bag. Make sure the zippers on your pack are strong and have a way to keep water and snow out (a flap or more commonly now, a waterproof zipper).

Hydration system: Many packs now have built-in hydration systems. I have seen these work with varying degrees of success in the winter. Some designs do not insulate the tube well enough to prevent freezing, while others seem to leak and cause problems. I have a pack where the water tube runs through my shoulder strap. In most conditions that is enough to keep the water unfrozen and allow me to hydrate easily. Your best bet is to talk to a salesperson or read reviews online to make sure the pack's hydration system is designed to withstand freezing temperatures.

Pack Fit

The critical thing to look for in a backpack of any size is a good fit. Here are some guidelines for checking fit:

Step 1: Loosen the shoulder straps and any other adjustments before putting the pack on. Load up the pack with some weight, approximately the amount of weight you anticipate carrying.

Step 2: Put the pack on your back, centering the hip belt on the top of your hipbones. Tighten the hip belt down snugly. The padded part of the hip belt should fit comfortably around your pelvic girdle, and you will want a couple of inches on either side of the buckle to allow you to make adjustments (or if you gain or lose weight!).

Step 3: Now snug down the shoulder straps so they wrap around your shoulders comfortably. The anchor point for the shoulder straps should fall an inch or two below the top of your shoulder.

Step 4: After the shoulders are tight, snug down the load-lifter straps if the pack has them. These are the straps on top of the shoulder straps that go back to the pack at a 45-degree angle and lift weight up off your shoulders.

Step 5: Once you adjust the load lifters, tighten the stabilizer straps, which attach to the outside of the hip belt. These straps pull the pack body close to the hip belt and stabilize the load. Not all packs will have these straps, however.

Step 6: Finally, you may want to ease the tension on your shoulder straps.

Once you have the pack adjusted, walk around. When you are snowshoeing or skiing with a pack, it's nice to have a pack that rides close to your body and moves with you so you don't get thrown off balance too easily. Make sure the weight is focused on your hips and you don't feel as if you are being pulled backward at your shoulders. This can be due to the way you've loaded the weight into the pack, but it can also mean the torso is too long, so the shoulder straps are too high.

Have someone look at the pack and make sure it fits well, or look in the mirror and check for strange angles or gaps. You'll be spending a lot of money on your pack, so it's worth making sure you have one that will be comfortable, durable, and accessible.

Overnight backpacks follow all the same principles listed above, except they need to be larger, which means you want to be extra sure they fit. A heavy, poorly fitting backpack hurts.

Sleds

For extended winter trips when you are carrying a lot of gear, food, and fuel, a sled can be a great asset. Sleds are pretty easy to pull on level and rolling terrain. They get trickier traversing slopes and kicking turns, but with practice, this becomes doable. Skiing downhill with a sled in powder can actually be pretty fun, or if the slope has a good run-out and your sled is well packed, you can just send it down the hill on its own. In trees? Well, depending on how tight the trees are, sleds can become a liability, but the beauty of a sled is that you can always strap it onto your backpack when conditions are too difficult to pull it.

Depending on your goals and pocketbook, you have a few options for sleds. You can add straps to a cheap plastic kiddie sled, or up the ante a bit by using plastic PVC pipe to create rigid poles. Or you can buy an expensive sled or pulk specifically designed for hauling gear.

Kiddie sleds are usually pulled with some kind of rope attached to the sled and tied into the hip belt of your backpack. These work just fine when you are moving forward over level, slightly uphill, or gently rolling terrain. They become a bit of a nuisance, however, when you

On longer trips, sleds are a great way to carry the food and equipment required to keep you warm and comfortable. ALLEN O'BANNON

are side-hilling—the sled slips out of the track and drags along below you . . . uncomfortable, awkward, and generally a pain. They are also tricky to ski downhill with because they tend to pass you by. But they work and can help you carry more gear than you want to carry on your back.

If you plan a lot of longer winter trips, a sled with rigid poles is preferred. Commercially made sleds with rigid aluminum poles and a waist harness work great, but they can be hard to find and expensive. You can make your own rigid poles on a kiddie sled by sliding two lengths of rope attached to the sled through PVC pipe approximately 5 feet long (long enough so your skis don't bang into the sled when you kick and glide along). Cross the poles in the middle for added control, and attach the straps to the hip belt of your pack with carabiners.

To control a sled with crossed rigid poles, use your hips. This becomes especially critical when traversing a slope where the sled wants to fall off the track and drag below you. Cock your uphill hip forward so the sled turns slightly uphill; this helps keep it tracking along behind you.

Winter Essentials
Shovel

A snow shovel is a critical piece of winter gear. With a shovel you can create a shelter, you can fill a pot with snow for making water, you can dig pits to analyze snow conditions, and if you have to, you can rescue your friends in an avalanche. You will want a shovel designed for winter use, rather than something from the hardware store. Buy one with a detachable, extendable handle for ease in packing and to save your back when you are digging. Get one with a metal blade so you can chop through hard, icy snow or avalanche debris.

Saw

If you are camping in the winter and plan to build snow shelters, a lightweight aluminum snow saw is a great tool. It enables you to cut blocks for capping shelters, building walls, etc. Snow saws are also nice for digging snow-study pits to assess conditions and evaluate the avalanche hazard.

Avalanche Safety Gear

Do you plan to be in terrain that has slopes of 30 degrees and up, or to hike up valleys that have slopes of 30 degrees or more above you? If so, you should be prepared for avalanches. I will talk more about avalanches later in the book; for now we'll focus on

A snow saw is useful for conducting stability tests to analyze the strength of the snowpack. It can also be helpful for cutting blocks to cap snow shelters or make walls. MOLLY ABSOLON

gear. If you answered yes to the questions above, you will want to carry, in addition to your shovel, an avalanche transceiver and an avalanche probe. However, just carrying this stuff is not enough. You need to know how to use it. We'll go into some details later, but this is my first plug for taking an avalanche course. It's a critical skill for winter travelers.

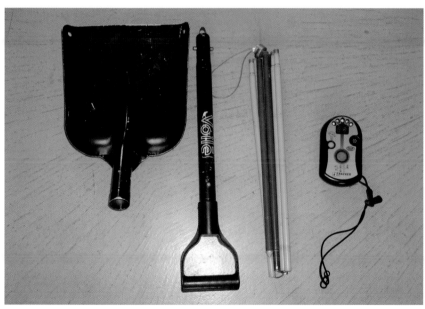

Anyone traveling in avalanche terrain should carry a minimum of a shovel, an avalanche probe, and a transceiver. MOLLY ABSOLON

Ice Ax

If your route involves ascending or descending steep snow, you should consider carrying an ice ax. You can create a handhold by shoving the ax down into the snow to give you stability and security. An ax also provides you with a way to stop yourself if you fall. Ice axes are not tools you can simply stick on your pack and know how to use, however. If you are planning to travel in conditions that require an ice ax, you should practice using it before you require those skills for your safety.

You can also buy an ice ax ski pole (Black Diamond sells one called a Whippet). These tools are designed for skiers who are climbing and skiing in terrain where a fall can be difficult to stop.

Crampons

Late season snow, early morning frozen snow, and glacial or alpine ice all require crampons to traverse securely. Crampons are metal-pronged plates that attach to the bottoms of your boots so you can walk across ice without slipping. Crampons can be highly technical for climbing waterfall ice, or they can be little more than ridged wires that you slap on to cross a small stretch of firm snow or ice in a parking lot. You can also buy ski crampons for use in the spring, when the snow is often frozen before the sun hits.

Repair Kits

Your equipment is critical to your well-being. If your skis break and you are 10 miles from the car, you face a long, arduous journey back to civilization. If your stove stops working, you no longer have a way to make water or cook your food. It is critical, therefore, to carry repair kits for all essential gear.

Depending on the length of your time outside and the distance you intend to travel, your repair kits will vary. For short trips I tend to have little more than some athletic tape, some duct tape, and a lightweight multi-tool or multi-bit screwdriver. As you get farther from the road, you need to carry more to cover yourself in case things go wrong, and remember, you have to actually know how to use this stuff. It doesn't help to carry a big repair kit if you have no idea what to do with the screws or splints.

In the appendix at the back of the book, you'll find a list of items to consider for your repair kit.

Shelters

Tents and Tarps

Tents are the simplest, fastest, and most convenient winter shelter. You just need to stamp out a tent platform, let the snow set up for ten or fifteen minutes, erect your shelter, and you are good to go. If you really want to get fancy, you can dig a trench in front of your door so you can sit with your feet dangling down outside to take off your boots.

For winter camping you need a four-season tent with poles and stitching strong enough to withstand a snow load, and enough guy lines to secure the tent firmly to the snow (see sidebar on deadman anchors).

A four-season tent is the quickest winter shelter to set up. MOE WITSCHARD

The only downsides to tents are they tend to be heavy and they aren't as warm as a snow shelter (or as quiet in a storm for that matter). But nothing beats the ease of throwing up a tent and crawling into bed.

Tarps can also work well in the winter. You can use a pyramid-style, single-pole tarp like the Black Diamond Megamid, or you can use a roof-shaped tarp strung between two trees. Tarps work best if you build walls around the sides and close in the bottom, making yourself a cozy, protected space to sleep.

A simple rectangular fly (top) can be made into a great winter shelter if you close in the sides with walls. Inside (bottom), you'll be warm, cozy, and protected from the wind. ALLEN O'BANNON

Make sure the tarp edge hangs over the top of the walls so that snow can slide off the outside rather than down into your shelter. Place a stuff sack or something under your center pole (if you have one) to keep it from plunging down into the snow.

Deadman Anchors

The best way to secure guy lines in the winter is with deadman anchors. First, gather up a handful of sticks about 6 inches long. Thumb-thick twigs work well, though really anything will suffice.

Dig a trench at a right angle to the guy line about 6 inches deep and wide enough for your stick. Take the guy line and lay it across the trench opening, put the stick on top of the line, and push both down to the bottom of the trench. The line should be underneath but not wrapped around the stick.

Bury your stick, making sure to keep both ends of the guy line uncovered. Stamp on the snow and then let it sit for five minutes to allow the snow to harden.

Once the snow is hard, take the guy line and tie it off to your shelter the same way you would with a line coming from a tent stake (using a taut line or trucker's hitch). You may need to run the string back and forth a bit under the deadman to free it up so you can make adjustments.

MOLLY ABSOLON

When you leave, there is no need to dig up the sticks—just pull the strings out and off you go.

Snow Shelters

We'll have a whole section on
snow shelters later in the book,
but here's a plug for them now:
If you are going winter camping,
you should sleep in a snow
shelter at least once in your life. It
can be raging outside—blizzard,
high winds, freezing cold temps—
and you'll be in an oasis of calm:
no wind, no snow, no sound,
and comfortable temperatures.
To build a shelter, you'll need a
minimum of a snow shovel.

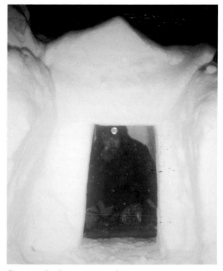

*Snow shelters provide a warm, cozy
sanctuary protected from the wind,
snow, and cold.* ALLEN O'BANNON

Yurts and Huts

Finally, in many mountainous parts of the world (Colorado, the Tetons,
British Columbia, New England, New Zealand, the Alps), there are

*Many mountainous parts of the world have hut systems that provide
comfortable shelters for winter travelers.* LYNNE WOLFE

alpine huts and yurts that you can stay in during the winter. These shelters can be a great way to get out and enjoy the winter environment with a bit more luxury in your accommodations.

Camping Equipment

If you do decide to camp out, there are a few things to know about gear that will be different from the summer.

Stoves, Lighters, and Pads

In cold temperatures white gas stoves work best. My personal favorite over the years has been the MSR Whisperlite. It's reliable and repairable, and the white gas it burns is usually easy to find and inexpensive. Mixed-fuel cartridges are great for convenience, but in general, these types of stoves don't work very well in cold temperatures, so I don't recommend them for winter camping. Other fuel types—alcohol, fuel tabs, wood—don't burn hot enough or quickly enough for winter camping.

I recommend carrying a lighter in a plastic bag in almost every pocket. I'll have one in my pants and one in my jacket, and maybe one in the top pocket of my pack. If you drop your lighter in the snow, it won't work for a while, hence the reason I like lots of backups.

You will need to have a pad for your stove to prevent it from melting down into the snow. A piece of plywood taped onto some closed-cell foam works well (the foam goes against the snow, not against the hot legs of the stove, which will melt it). Or you can use a piece of aluminum. You'll want a pot pad too, to keep your pot from sinking down into the snow when you remove it from the stove.

Fuel

In the winter you can't always find running water. Everything is frozen, which means you have to melt snow to drink. I'll go into more detail about melting snow later, but for now, recognize you'll need more fuel in the winter than you do in the summer to ensure you have adequate water. Typically a group of two or three uses about ⅓ liter of white gas a day in the summer, depending on the type of food they are cooking. In the winter that same group will probably use up to ¾ liter of fuel per day, mainly because of the fuel required to melt snow.

Pots, Skillets, and Utensils
Nothing too earth-shattering here. You just need your regular cooking gear. However, because you are constantly making water as well as cooking food, you will want two large pots for a group of three (you may also want two stoves).

Lanterns
Days are short in the winter, especially in December and January, so it's nice to have a lantern. A candle lantern or small white gas lantern works great and can add some homey cheer to your dark campsite. Remember, don't take a lantern or stove into your snow shelter. The airflow inside a snow cave or qhinzee is not sufficient to prevent carbon monoxide poisoning, so beware. Candle lanterns are fine inside a shelter.

Flashlights and Spare Batteries
Because of winter's long, dark nights, flashlights are essential. Lithium batteries work best in the cold, lasting much longer than regular batteries. Nonetheless, if you plan to be out for a week or more, bring spare batteries to ensure you aren't left in the dark

Sleeping Systems
You will need a winter sleeping bag. Ratings for the bag will depend on where you plan to travel. In many parts of the country, a bag rated to –30°F is needed for comfortable sleeping in the winter; in other parts you can be comfortable in a 0° bag. Take into consideration your own body temperature. Many people sleep either warm or cold and therefore will need to go with a warmer or colder bag to be comfortable. You can also use a less-warm bag and wear your insulating clothes to sleep in to bring up the R-value. The idea that you need to sleep naked to sleep warm is rubbish; however, sleeping in too many clothes can be restrictive and uncomfortable.

You lose a lot of heat through conduction if you don't have adequate insulation underneath your sleeping bag. It's nice to have one thick full-length pad. (Therm-a-Rests or inflatable pads are great, but be sure to carry a repair kit because you'll be hating life if your pad goes flat and you have no way to fix it.) In addition, I like to bring a half-pad made from closed-cell foam to boost the insulation under me while sleeping, and also to give me something to sit and stand on while hanging out in camp. You can put clothes you aren't wearing or your pack underneath you as well. Anything that keeps you from contact with the snow will help keep you extra warm.

Personal Items
Toiletries
You really don't need much more than a toothbrush and a tiny tube of toothpaste. If you wear contact lenses, bring the minimum amount of contact solution you need and carry it in a pouch around your neck or a pocket close to your body to prevent it from freezing. Don't forget sunscreen and lip balm.

Pee Bottle
A wide-mouth Nalgene bottle or bowl with a screw-on lid works great as a pee bottle for both boys and girls. You may think "gross," but give it a try. You spend a lot of time in bed in the winter, so inevitably you will need to pee before it's time to get up. Having a pee bottle keeps you from having to get into all your clothes to go outside. That said, there are definitely stories of spilled pee bottles, and for women, it may take a little practice if you have never used one before (but if you can pee into the cup at the doctor's office, you can pee into a pee bottle, no problem).

Water Bottles
Wide-mouth bottles are better in the winter than water bottles with narrow openings, because they are easier to fill and harder to freeze shut. Nalgene bottles are durable and stand up well to freezing temperatures. Cheap, thin plastic bottles can shatter or crack in extreme cold.

Sunglasses, Goggles, and Bandana or Cloth

You will probably want both sunglasses and goggles for winter travel. Goggles are critical when it's stormy and you need to protect your eyes. Sunglasses are critical on bright, sunny days when the glare off the snow threatens to burn your corneas (snow blindness). It's a good idea to have a cotton bandana or cloth to wipe off the glasses and goggles.

CHAPTER 4

Living in the Snow

Know Snow

Part of learning to live and recreate in the winter involves understanding some basic principles about snow. Snow falls from the sky as a crystal. Each crystal is unique, although there are several distinctive forms, including the classic snowflake, which is called a stellar. Other forms include graupel, columns, needles, and spatial dendrites. Once these crystals hit the ground, they begin to change. Depending on the ambient air temperature and the depth of the snowpack, that metamorphism can make the snow better for traveling, camping, or skiing, or it can make it worse.

When you have a low snowpack and cold temperatures, the snow begins to facet, meaning the crystals transform themselves into big, cup-shaped grains. These facets are what many people call "sugar" snow. They have no bonds between the different grains and as a result are difficult, if not impossible, to get to stick together. Facets make building snow shelters or kitchens and setting a good track for hiking, snowshoeing, or skiing almost impossible. They also do not bode well for avalanche stability.

When temperatures are more moderate and the snowpack deep and well insulated, crystals morph into rounded grains that form necks linking the individual grains together. The result is a strong, well-bonded snowpack that forms perfect snowballs, kitchen counters, trails, and shelters.

Well-bonded snow allows you to create kitchen counters, seats, stairs, and snow shelters that make living out in the winter comfortable. ALLEN O'BANNON

Campsite Selection

When you look for a campsite, try to find a spot out of the bottom of a valley or drainage, since cold air sinks. Think about sunlight. I prefer maximizing my morning sun. I love feeling that sun warm and cheer me up as it pokes up over the horizon and touches down on my kitchen, so I look for an east-facing exposure for my camp. You'll also want protection from the wind. Try tucking in behind a hill or by a clump of trees to get some shelter.

You want to consider safety as well. Don't plop yourself down at the base of a potential avalanche slope. Increasingly, dead trees are an issue in the Rocky Mountains due to beetle kill. It can be hard to avoid dead trees altogether, so it's worth pushing on them to see if they are strong. That knowledge may help you sleep better if the wind comes up at night.

Otherwise, there's not much to think about in a winter campsite. You can shovel it flat, so it doesn't matter if you are on a slope. Your water source is all around you, and snow covers rocks and bushes, so you can really plop yourself down just about anywhere.

Getting Settled Down

Winter camping is the most fun when you work together to get the chores done. There's a lot to do when you pull into camp: You need to make your shelter or set up your tent; you'll probably need to make water and food; you need to organize your belongings so things don't get lost in the snow; and you need to take care of yourself so you don't get cold. So where do you begin?

Start by divvying up the tasks. Assign someone to take charge of getting the stove going, making water, and preparing food or hot drinks. Shovel out a temporary kitchen. You really just need a small, work-hardened surface for your stove. Change out of your damp traveling clothes into warm, dry gear as you work. Make sure to put on dry socks as quickly as you can so your feet don't get cold. Damp clothing should be hung on your body (socks draped over shoulders or tucked into the waistband of your pants, for example) so that it begins to dry or at least doesn't freeze while you work.

Another person can begin making your camp. This may simply involve stamping out a tent platform and changing into warm clothes

When setting up or breaking down camp, divvy up chores to maximize efficiency and minimize time. JERAMIE PRINE

while the platform sets up, or you may need to stomp out a foundation for your snow shelter (or find a good snowdrift to dig into) and then begin mounding snow. Again, one or two people can be doing this while another is making food and water.

A critical part of enjoyable, efficient winter camping is "bombproofing." The term comes from NOLS's founder, Paul Petzoldt, who demanded his students' camps were organized and clean enough to withstand a proverbial bombing. Petzoldt was said to go around acting as a kind of storm to ingrain these habits into his students. He'd pour water in boots left outside and hide clothing that was inappropriately stored. His tactics may have been harsh, but the message was invaluable. Your gear is part of your safety system, especially in the winter. If you lose something or an item becomes unusable because it's frozen or broken, at best it's an inconvenience, at worst it may actually jeopardize your life.

So part of getting camp set up is making sure everything you are not using is stored away properly. Skis lying on the ground disappear under piles of snow as you build your shelters or dig out a kitchen. And a ski pole left stuck into the snow gets frozen in place, so you lose your basket when you pull it free. Instead, stick your skis upright in the snow and hang your poles off of them. Try to keep everything else in a duffel or your pack, in your shelter, or carefully organized in your kitchen. Lean your sled or snowshoes against a tree. The fewer places you have to look for things, the easier it is to find everything if you get a foot of snow overnight.

Snow Shelters and Kitchens
Qhinzees

Qhinzee is the Athabascan name for a snow shelter made from piled-up snow. The Athabascan people generally live in the interior of Alaska where the snowpack is thin and the temperatures cold. In these conditions it can be hard to find snowbanks to dig into for shelter, so people were forced to build their own mound of snow to carve out. Qhinzees can be built in relatively low snow conditions, but the thinner

Mound up snow for your qhinzee (above) around loaded duffel bags. When you hollow out your dome, the duffels will mean you have to move less snow.

Poles and skis stuck into the qhinzee (left) help give you a guide on wall thickness. Ideally a qhinzee's walls are around 16 inches thick.

Home, sweet home (left).
ALLEN O'BANNON

the pack, the more snow you will have to transport to make a shelter of any size. In snow conditions deeper than, say, 4 feet, you probably want to go with a different type of shelter that does not involve building a mound.

The size of your qhinzee will depend on your group size, but a good place to start is to make the diameter of the circle twice the length of your skis. After you've ski-stamped the area, take off your skis and boot-pack around the perimeter. This will really compress the snow and give you a firm foundation for whatever structure you intend to construct. To speed things up, you can pile some duffel bags into the center of your circle to take up some space. (Don't put things inside that you might need in the next couple of hours. It will be a while before you see the duffels again.) Then start tossing snow into a pile.

Work-Hardened Snow

If you've made a snowball, you've work-hardened snow. You have experienced how pressing snow together in your hands changes it, compressing the spaces between the grains and allowing the crystals to bond together more strongly. There's some magic involved that we don't need to go into. Suffice it to say, if you want to build things with snow, you need to work-harden it first; otherwise, the powder will just collapse as you carve. The amount of work-hardening required depends on the quality of the snow. Sugary, faceted snow bonds very poorly and takes a long time to work-harden. I know people who mound up this kind of snow for a shelter and let it sit overnight before starting to dig in. Powdery, new snow bonds much more quickly, as does wet, warm snow.

To be on the safe side, stomp out the area you plan to use with your skis. You can stand in the middle and spin around in place stamping as you go, or sidestep across to form a square. The size and shape will depend on what you are building. Now start shoveling. Mound up snow for a shelter and pile it up for kitchen counters, smack your pile with a shovel, and then let it sit while you change your boots, put on a layer, and have a hot drink. After you've given the snow time to bond, go back and try carving out a spot. If the snow holds together, you're ready to go. If it crumbles under your touch, you need to give it more time to harden.

Your desired shape is a big gumdrop. You want a nice domed top with steep sides. Depending on how deep the snow is, you'll want a mound that rises about 4 to 6 feet above your foundation.

Once you get your dome piled up, shape and smooth it by smacking the snow with your shovel. This is a great time to take out any aggressions or frustrations you might have. Beat that thing. The more work-hardening you do, the stronger your shelter.

Now take a break. Give the snow time to bond—usually this means allowing the mound to sit for an hour or two minimum.

When the snow is ready, stick everyone's skis and poles into the pile about 18 to 24 inches deep, transforming your mound into a kind of pincushion. The skis and poles will serve as markers for the "mole," or individual hollowing out the mound. When he or she hits a ski or pole, it indicates the wall is about 18 to 24 inches thick at that spot. In general, you want your walls to be about 16 inches thick. Too much thinner or thicker than that, and the walls will sag more quickly over time.

Now it's time to start digging. "Moling" out a qhinzee is a two-person job. You need one individual to stand by the doorway, moving away snow and keeping tabs on the person inside. And you need one person inside, hollowing out the shelter. I recommend this person wear minimal clothes: probably base layers, wind gear, a hat and gloves, and boots. You'll get wet both from the exercise and from lying in the snow, so the less you have on, the better.

Begin by carving out a door. Again, you are looking for a nice arched shape. Remember learning in art history that an arch is the strongest form in nature? Well, keep that in mind as you dig. Do everything in curves. That shape is key to your safety and the longevity of the shelter. Flat-topped qhinzees can collapse on you.

The size of your door depends on your personal preference. Smaller doors make it more awkward to get in and out of your shelter and harder to move the snow out as you dig, but they are warmer. Bigger doors make moving around easier, but can be drafty and cold. So start with a door high enough to allow you to sit on your knees to shovel, maybe with your head ducked down. The door's width should be about as wide as your shoulders with a few extra inches to spare.

The mole will hollow his or her way back about 2 feet and then start digging up. I like to carve out a space where my arms and shoulders can move more freely once I get back into the interior of the qhinzee. It can be rather cramped and claustrophobic in the door tunnel.

Once you can stand up, start shaving down from the top with your shovel. Make your walls smooth and, again, think of that gumdrop shape. You want nice steep walls and an arched ceiling. Eventually you'll uncover the duffels you left inside. Push those out to your doorkeeper and heave a big sigh of relief. The duffels save you time and energy by cutting down on the amount of snow you have to excavate.

Moling takes a while. You'll have to shave snow off the ceiling and then shovel it out to your door person. It helps to stay hydrated and fed while you work. You may want to take breaks or trade off the moling duties—just be careful when you come outside that you don't get chilled. You'll be warm and wet and will need to change into dry clothing quickly to avoid getting cold.

Qhinzees can collapse if the snow is not adequately bonded together. A collapsed qhinzee is like a small avalanche. Your mole may be trapped under a couple of feet of snow and could potentially suffocate if you don't get him or her out quickly. To avoid this possibility, always have someone

The inside of a qhinzee is quiet, warm, cozy, and away from the blustery weather outside. ALLEN O'BANNON

at the door watching to make sure the mole is safe. And if the mole hears the shelter collapse or go *whumpf* without actually falling down, he or she should back out and let the snow set up for a while longer.

To finish up the qhinzee, poke a few holes through the walls with a ski pole to serve as vents for allowing moisture to escape. Carve out some alcoves for your personal belongings or candles, and then smooth out the floor. If you have adequate snow, make a sleeping platform that is raised above the level of the door. This will create a heat trap and maximize the warmth of your shelter. If the snow is not deep enough, don't worry: Your shelter will still be plenty warm, and you can always block the door with duffel bags to keep heat from escaping.

Snow caves

If you have adequate snow, you don't need to pile up a mound, you can just dig a snow cave. Ideally you'll want to find a snowdrift that is 6 feet deep or more. Probe around to make sure there are no hidden rocks or stumps before you commit to digging. Once you are satisfied, go to the face or steep side of the drift and tunnel in. You'll follow the same basic principles you followed for moling out a qhinzee: Carve out a small door; go back a couple of feet before digging up; use nice arcing, shaving motions to carve out the space; have a door person to spot and move snow; and wear minimal clothes. It's pretty basic. Again, go for the gumdrop shape inside.

The only real downside to snow caves is the fact that where you get big enough drifts to dig into, you have lots of wind, so good snow cave sites may not make great kitchen sites. If it's too blustery and stormy outside your door to cook, you can either make an indoor kitchen by carving an alcove out of the snowdrift, or you can build your kitchen somewhere more sheltered. The wind won't affect you when you are inside.

Digloos

Digloos are a variation of both a qhinzee and a snow cave. The big difference is that you not only hollow in from the bottom, you also dig down from the top. This speeds up the moling process because you can have two people digging at the same time. The person coming down from the top creates a kind of vertical tube with a circumference of 3 feet or less (the smaller it is, the easier it is to cap—more on that later). You probably want to have your shovel handle retracted at first so you can work in this confined space. Once you've dug down about 14 to 16 inches, you can start arcing out. Eventually you'll be able to stand in the opening, gradually working your way down. Make sure to retain a pedestal in the

Quarrying

Digloos require snow blocks to close off the hole in the roof. To make blocks, you need to establish a quarry. First, stamp out an area one ski-length long and about a pole-length wide. Let the snow stand for an hour or two to work-harden.

Once the snow is set, carve out a vertical face to the front of your quarry. The face should be the height of your snow saw blade, which is usually about 18 inches long. Now you can cut blocks from the quarry. Make each block the height of your snow saw blade; the length of the entire snow saw (including handle), or about 2 feet long; and as thick as the snow saw handle, or about 5 inches wide. Often the first blocks are the hardest to cut out and may crumble. Don't throw the broken pieces away; you may be able to use them to chink in your cap.

After you ski- and boot-stamp your quarry, let it sit until the snow hardens. Then cut your blocks using a snow saw. The first blocks will often crumble, but farther back in the quarry, they'll be harder. MOLLY ABSOLON

center of your floor so you can continue to reach the opening at the top. You'll need to stand on this pedestal to cap your shelter.

To cap your digloo, you'll need two to four blocks, plus some of the broken bits and pieces to fill in the gaps. If the hole in the top of your digloo is small, you can just lean two blocks together in an inverted V shape and fill in the gaps with your chinking materials. If the hole is too big for this technique, you'll want to lean three blocks together to form a tripod shape. You'll need one person inside the digloo standing on the snow pedestal you left on the floor, while another person is outside passing blocks up. It helps to have a tall person who can lean the first block against his or her shoulder on the inside to get things started. Your goal is to balance the blocks on the corners—don't try to get the entire edge flush with either the digloo roof or the other blocks. Once the three blocks are perched in place, you can cut a smaller block to cap the open space between the blocks. Then just fill in the holes on the sides, and you are good to go.

Lean blocks in at as steep an angle as possible, balancing them at the corners. You can support the initial blocks with your shoulders and back.

Putting in the last block.

Finished cap. ALLEN O'BANNON

Doghouses

Made from a simple trench with blocks lined up for a roof, a doghouse is a quick solo shelter that works well in an emergency or for those nights when you want some privacy. To make a doghouse, excavate a rectangular trench in the snow just wide enough for you to lie in comfortably. The wider the trench, the harder it is to cap, so keep that in mind as you dig. Dig down deep enough so you can sit up comfortably.

Once your trench is complete, cap it by leaning snow blocks (you'll need a quarry for blocks) against each other over the top of the trench, creating an A-frame roof. It's easiest if you zipper or offset the blocks as you set them up so. It's also easier if you have someone help by passing blocks to you; otherwise, stack them up at one end of your trench so you can reach them without having to climb out.

If you don't feel like making blocks, you can cap your shelter with a tarp. The only downside is the tarp will be flat and will fill up with snow if you get a storm overnight.

Emergency Shelters

Snow caves and doghouses can be used as emergency shelters. All you need to construct them is a shovel and the proper snow conditions. In the absence of these two factors, tree wells make an adequate shelter, particularly if you can find a hollow under some big overhanging branches. To beef up the shelter, you can drape a tarp over the top, or just hunker down in all your clothes.

Snow Kitchens

Oftentimes the best place to start your kitchen is in the mounds of snow coming out of your snow shelter. But if you aren't making a snow shelter, just pile up snow and let it sit for a while before starting to excavate your kitchen.

The most basic and functional kitchen shape is a horseshoe. Carve out counters at just the right height for your comfort, leaving a wall of snow behind to block the wind. Kick in the bottom of the counter to create space for your toes. Make some benches. Designate an area of

Snow counters allow you to stand up while you cook. ALLEN O'BANNON

clean snow for your water supply. You'll also want to designate a sump hole for your wastewater, making sure the two don't mix for sanitary purposes.

Carve out alcoves to store kitchen items: a shelf for food bags and stoves, for example. You will also need to make a water storage spot, typically a carved-out section under your counter where you can store pots of water overnight. That water will stay unfrozen if you put it into the snow and close off the space with either your food bags or a block of snow.

Indoor kitchens can be great in stormy weather, but they need

Make a hole in your counter to store your water overnight. You can cover the hole with a block of snow or a food bag. This way you'll have liquid water rather than solid ice to start off your morning. ALLEN O'BANNON

to be constructed with plenty
of ventilation to prevent carbon
monoxide poisoning. Make the
door tall enough to walk through
(unlike the low, warmth-retaining
door you construct for a sleeping
shelter), and put a chimney or
a large hole in the roof for air to
escape. You can cap the hole
loosely with blocks—don't chink
in the spaces and cracks—if the
weather is stormy and you are
getting lots of spindrift coming in
through the roof.

If you are making a snow
shelter and want an indoor
kitchen, use the snow you

*You can make an alcove out of snow (top) to make a covered kitchen area or
use a fly (bottom) to cover your kitchen and keep out the weather.* ALLEN O'BANNON

excavate from inside the shelter to pile up for your kitchen. I had a shelter once where we constructed a small tunnel between our kitchen and the qhinzee for passing food and drinks back and forth. That meant one of us could be in the kitchen cooking, while the others were in their sleeping bags drinking hot cocoa and eating dinner.

Organization

Life in the winter is much easier if you are organized and efficient. If you develop a system for your equipment, for where to put things, and for who does which chores, life will flow smoothly and enjoyably. But if you are disorganized, you are likely to lose things, be uncomfortable, get resentful, and end up hating life.

In your kitchen, make sure you consolidate your belongings. A cool spice rack is nice while you are cooking, but if you leave your spices lined out on the counter and it snows overnight, you are unlikely to ever find the salt again. Close up your kitchen at the end of a meal by putting everything away.

Fill your stove with fuel after each meal—there's nothing quite so annoying as getting water halfway to boiling and having the stove sputter out, especially when it's 20 below and you haven't had your coffee yet. Before you put away your stove, make sure everyone has a full water bottle, and before bed, leave a pot full of water ready for breakfast.

Going to Bed

Getting into bed is a bit of an ordeal. There's lots of organizing, fluffing, and moving around that goes into making yourself comfortable and ready to sleep, so I recommend one person get into bed at a time. That prevents most elbowing and bumping and lost gear.

Send one member of your party into the shelter to get into bed while another shuts down camp for the night. Start by making sure you are warm before you crawl into your bag. Remember, insulation comes from warm dead air space, but the only way to warm the dead

Helpful Hints

Liquids freeze in the winter without a furnace to keep the temperature up, so make sure you insulate the things you don't want to freeze.

It's much, much harder to thaw a liter block of ice than to keep your water bottle from freezing. I carry my water bottle inside an insulated bootie. You can also wrap it in Ensolite or buy a premade insulated case. Stick the bottle down into your pack so it's protected a bit from the cold external air temperatures. It can help to tip the bottle upside down, since typically things start to freeze on the top, and if the bottle is inverted, you won't have as much trouble getting a frozen lid off. You can also start with warm water in the morning to slow the cooling rate.

Drape damp socks over your shoulders or tuck them into the waistband of your long underwear to keep them warm and facilitate drying. When you are cooking, hold the warm pot with your damp wool gloves to help them dry.

In the days of leather ski boots, it was imperative that you sleep with your boots to keep them from turning into blocks of ice by morning. Nowadays most winter boots come with a removable liner, so you only need to sleep with the inner boots at night. Many boots have thermal liners that don't absorb water, which means you can get away without sleeping with them at all. Basically the worst you'll find in the morning is some frost on the outside of the liners that can be brushed off easily. That said, unfrozen doesn't mean warm. If you tend to have cold feet like me, sleeping with your liners helps keep them from getting really cold. Or if you have plenty of fuel, you can make hot water bottles in the morning and stick them in your boot liners to warm them up until it's time to put your boots on. Finally, chemical hand and foot warmers are a nice luxury for those really cold days.

air space in your sleeping bag is with your body, so go to bed with your internal furnace cranking. Eat a good dinner. Winter is the time you can allow yourself to eat lots of fats without worry. You are burning plenty of calories just staying warm, let alone hiking, skiing, shoveling . . . so eat a big, fattening dinner and rev up your engine. Next, when you are about to go to bed, take a quick jog or ski around camp to get your muscles moving. Exercise is your best way to get warm. Make sure you pee right before you go inside your shelter.

The first step to getting into bed is to remove all snow from your body. This snow will melt in the warmth of your shelter, making things wet, so it's important to get it off outside rather than bringing it into your sanctuary. A small whiskbroom can be helpful in this endeavor, especially with boots, where the snow can be icy and resistant to a simple brush-off.

Now put down your sleeping pads. I make sure my half-pad is under my torso, so I have a double layer of padding where I'm likely to lose the most heat. I then place my insulated parka and pants on top of the pads to put yet another layer between the snow and me. If you tend to have cold feet, you may want to wrap your parka around your feet, or better yet, make a hot water bottle.

I sleep in my long underwear and a pile sweater or jacket, and I put on socks designated for sleeping and wear booties. A hat is essential. If your sleeping bag is not warm enough, don't hesitate to put on your parka or insulated pants.

The only downside to winter camping is dealing with your damp clothes. Without a dryer, your body is the heater that is going to dry this stuff (although the sun does a remarkable job, so make sure to hang things out when it's sunny and you are in camp), which means you have to sleep with it. I put socks and gloves between my torso and the ground, where I am generating the most heat. Some people like to put them on their thighs. Most keep their damp clothing inside their sleeping bags, but I don't. I tend to sleep cold and find having damp clothing in my bag chills me. So I put my wet stuff outside my bag, between the sleeping bag and pad. That said, my socks and gloves do not dry out by morning using this method. They are, however, warm, so I can put them on and dry them out by wearing them. You decide. I know lots of people who sleep really warm and can dry out just about anything in their sleeping bag. But I'm a wimp . . . and a cold sleeper.

Some people also like to sleep with a snack in case they get cold and hungry during the night. You can make a little cubby near your head if you are in a snow shelter or have a small stuff sack with snacks and a headlamp handy in case you wake up in the dark and need light and food.

And you should know, you will wake up in the night. Long winter nights mean long hours prone in your bag. Inevitably you'll need to pee or shift your body or change your layers. Don't fight it. The urge to pee will not go away with willpower. Get up, go out, and pee, and you'll still have plenty of time to sleep. If you get cold, do some sit-ups in your bag or have a snack. Relax, and don't fret about being awake.

Airing Out Your Sleeping Bag

You often will find your bag is damp in the morning. There's lots of moisture coming out of your body and from the clothes you are drying in your bag, so if you have time in the morning, bring your bag out to air. Stick your skis into the snow and hang your sleeping bag between them with the zipper open. If the sun is out, the bag will dry quickly. But even if it's overcast, the moisture will evaporate, especially in a breeze. This method also works when it's snowing as long as it's not a warm, wet snow. You'll know the difference: If snow is melting on your jacket, it's too wet to air out your bag. If it just falls there and can be brushed off without leaving any moisture, evaporation will still work.

Sleeping bags get damp from condensation during the night, so it's important to hang your bag out to dry in the morning. ALLEN O'BANNON

Using the Bathroom

Peeing in the winter is easy. If you have to go, you go. Ideally in camp you'll designate a urinal of sorts. This ensures you don't inadvertently contaminate your water supply, and also keeps your camp from looking like a pack of huskies has been marking its territory everywhere.

I do use a pee bottle at night because I hate crawling out of my shelter once I'm warm and cozy. There's no rocket science to using a pee bottle, but I suggest you practice at least once before you try it in the dark with lots of layers on. The main dangers are bad aim and improper closure (and maybe stage fright if you have tentmates in close quarters). Either of those failures is pretty bad—a urine-soaked sleeping bag is a big bummer in the winter. So if in doubt about your skills, crawl outside and do your business in the great outdoors.

Defecating in the winter is a little bit controversial because it's usually impossible to make your deposit in the dirt where it will be covered up and broken down by bacteria. In the winter the dirt is frozen and inaccessible under snow, but if you happen to be out and about where you can get to earth and are able to make a hole, by all means do. The best practice for depositing your feces in the outdoors continues to be the cathole: a 6-inch-deep hole in the dirt where you leave your deposit.

Actually, that is not entirely true: The best technique for leaving no trace is really to pack your poop out. There are a number of products (WAG bags, Restop, etc.) on the market designed to allow you to carry your waste out of the backcountry and deposit it into a trashcan. These bags are a great way to make sure your feces are disposed of properly.

In the absence of dirt or the feasibility of a WAG bag, you are left with burying your waste in the snow. Give yourself time to do your business. You'll want to put on your skis or snowshoes so you can get away from water, camp, or the trail—200 feet is a good distance. I used to tell students to think about their pacing. Most of us average around 3- or 4-foot paces (more or less depending on your height), so on average you are going to want to go about 70 paces from camp, water, or trails. Obviously, water is usually frozen, but you still want to move away from lakeshores or drainages because once the snow melts, your feces will be exposed and can get into the water.

Stomp out an area in the snow before you drop trou. You may then want to remove skis or snowshoes, depending on your stability and ability to spread your legs wide enough to ensure a clean deposit. No one wants "brown klister" on his skis. Punch a hole 6 or so inches deep in the middle of your platform with your ski pole, and you are good to go. Ideal sites are located near trees, where it tends to be warmer, accelerating decomposition in the spring. Trees also give you something to hang on to if you want support in your squat.

Some people advocate snow for toilet paper. You can mold snowballs to the perfect body-conforming shape if you have the right type of snow. The advantage to snow is it cleans as it wipes, which is nice in the winter when bathing is impossible. But snow is cold and can be uncomfortable, so you may want to bring yourself some TP. You'll just have to pack it out with you, which isn't that big a deal if you double bag it in plastic. Remember, too, everything is frozen, which means odor is not a problem.

After you finish, cover your deposit with snow. You don't have to bury it too deeply—in fact, the warmth of the sun is crucial to the feces' eventual decomposition—but you also don't want your teammates or others following behind you to accidently encounter your poop. Yuck.

Make sure to wash your hands thoroughly after you defecate. You can take snow and rub it vigorously in your hands to wash them. The snow will melt as you scrub, so your hands will be wet. Or you may want to consider carrying hand sanitizer for this purpose.

CHAPTER 5

Winter Cuisine

When you think about food for winter hiking and camping, think lots of calories and not much prep. In general, you are going to want immediate—or nearly immediate—gratification when hunger calls. You also need to think about what works well in the cold; for example, certain bars get so hard, they can break your teeth, making them less than ideal winter trail food.

At NOLS, the winter ration contains between 3,500 and 5,000 calories per day, which equates to 2 to 2.5 pounds per person per day. This may seem like a lot of food, especially when you consider that the recommended daily caloric intake for adult males is around 2,000 calories per day. The difference has to do with your energy output. In the winter you are burning calories like mad whether you are shoveling, walking, skiing, or just trying to stay warm. You need the added fuel to ensure you have enough BTUs to sustain yourself throughout the day and the night. So eat with abandon. You'll burn the calories.

Day Food

I am a big fan of carrying a thermos on winter day tours. Whether you fill it with soup, tea, or hot chocolate is up to you, but for me there's nothing that goes down quite as easily as warm liquids. Cold water can be hard to swallow in burly (or stormy) weather, so having something warm will also help you stay hydrated.

Otherwise, I don't think there's too much difference between trail food in the summer and trail food in the winter. You may discover you find certain foods more or less palatable in the cold. I personally like sandwiches, cheese, crackers, and summer sausage more than bags of trail food. I think I crave the fat, salt, and protein. But you may lean toward sweeter things.

Just remember:

It's important to stay hydrated in the winter. On warm days, water is fine. On cold days, a thermos with something hot tends to go down easier. MOLLY ABSOLON

- Excessively hard or chewy foods can be difficult to eat when cold or frozen. It helps to carry these kinds of foods in a pocket next to your body to keep them soft. Or just avoid them altogether.

- Wrappers are a nuisance in the winter, so unwrap candy and bars at home to avoid accidental littering.

- Keep snacks handy so you can eat all day to avoid hitting the wall. Stay hydrated.

Overnight Food

Winter camping involves plenty of chores to keep you busy around camp—plus there's always the untracked powder beckoning you to come play—so I prefer simple, fast meals when camping in winter. That means foods like mac and cheese, beans and rice with cheese, cheesy potatoes, chili with cheese, and spaghetti with cheese are popular

Cheesy, high-calorie, one-pot meals are easy to prepare and provide lots of calories to keep you going. ALLEN O'BANNON

winter menu items. Note the emphasis on cheese. Cheese is a great source of calories and fat in the winter, so I tend to throw it into just about everything. Obviously, not everyone likes cheese. If you don't like or can't eat cheese, consider other options that will give you the calories and fat you need, such as nut butters.

Breakfasts should be equally hearty: hash browns with cheese, buttery hot cereal, bacon, fried bagels with cheese or peanut butter, and other high-calorie foods give you a boost in the morning.

Instant mashed potatoes or Cup-a-Soups, ramens, miso, and other soup mixes make good afternoon snacks or lunchtime pick-me-ups when packed along in a thermos. To boost their caloric value, add—you guessed it—cheese! And you'll want to pack lots of hot drink options like assorted tea bags and hot chocolate. Hot spiced milk—using milk powder, ginger, sugar, and nutmeg or cinnamon—can be a fun alternative to hot chocolate.

Some people like to bring a little liquor for a hot toddy at night. The one thing to remember with alcohol is that it actually dehydrates you, so drink it with care in the backcountry. Too much alcohol not only affects your ability to take care of yourself, it can also affect your body's ability to stay warm.

Winter temperatures mean you can bring frozen food, so pack in a frozen pizza, a bag of frozen vegetables, or meat if you like. You can prepare a meal at home, freeze it, and then reheat it in the field. Frozen food is heavy, so this option is really best suited for trips where you are pulling a sled and weight is not a concern. But on long expeditions, it's kind of nice to have vegetables or a hamburger for dinner.

Prepping Food in Town

On the plus side, winter temperatures allow food to keep indefinitely. On the down side, it's hard to work with a big chunk of frozen cheese. So it's a good idea to chop things up into manageable sizes before you leave the warmth of your home. Cube your cheese to make it easier to work with, and cut meat and butter into small pieces. Remove excess packaging so you don't have to deal with lots of trash.

You might consider organizing your food before you go out to make life easier. For example, you can carry all the food for one day of the trip in one bag, while your partner carries the next day's food in another bag. A different way to organize food is to have a breakfast bag, a lunch and drink bag, and a dinner bag. Any method works—it is just useful to find some kind of system to limit the amount of time you spend digging around for a bag of cocoa or instant soup packets.

Cooking Tips

Winter camping is all about tricks, or knowing the little things that make your life a whole lot easier. For example, if you leave your lighter in your stove bag in the winter like I normally do in the summer, it gets damp and cold and will not work. So, I carry a lighter in my pocket in a plastic bag so it stays dry and works when I need it when I'm winter camping.

Other tricks include covering your stove with an overturned pot at night to prevent snow from getting down into it and freezing the moving parts so it doesn't work in the morning. You can also put the stove into a pot bag to protect it from the elements.

Wear light wool gloves around the kitchen, especially when filling the stove. Gas can become supercooled, causing contact frostbite if it touches bare skin. Use a funnel to prevent spilling, and make sure to refuel well away from your water-supply snow. Unlike urine, gas leaves no telltale color indicating where it has been spilled.

Lighting Stoves in the Cold

Stoves can be persnickety in the cold, so you need to baby them a bit. Mainly that means making sure to keep them out of the snow and allowing them to prime for an adequate length of time. When temps

Don't be afraid to use a lot of liquid fuel to prime your stove. You need to make sure it is heated up enough to vaporize the gas, and when temperatures are cold, that process takes longer and requires more fuel than when temperatures are warm. MOLLY ABSOLON

drop well below freezing, fuel can be hard to light. The trick is to warm up your fuel. One way to do this is to sleep with the fuel in your shelter. Another way is to warm the spirit cup—the metal cup at the base of the stove that you fill with liquid fuel to prime the stove—with a lighter.

Once you have done this, pour fuel into the spirit cup. Fill it to the brim and light the fuel. This will be more fuel than you normally use for priming your stove, so you'll have a bit of a campfire going for a while, but in cold temps it helps to ensure you warm up the stove enough to vaporize the liquid gas completely. You have probably dealt with a stove that's caught in between temperatures, causing the fuel to come out in a combination of gas and liquid. It's a pain: The fuel flares up, you can't start cooking, and you basically end up having to wait until the stove cools down to start over again. So make sure to get the stove well primed before you try lighting it.

In the winter it's especially helpful to be organized in the kitchen, since turning the stove off and on is bothersome and a waste of gas. Stoves quickly cool down, meaning you'll have to prime it every time you turn it on again, which is time-consuming and inefficient. So be

To conserve fuel, cook with a windscreen in a protected spot. ALLEN O'BANNON

ready and keep the stove burning until you are done. That means having the ingredients of your meal laid out on the counter, ready to go.

Other ways to maximize the stove's performance is to use a windscreen or build a protected alcove for the stove with snow. And always use a lid when you are cooking to prevent heat from escaping into the atmosphere.

Making Water

You may be able to camp next to an open stream or lake, but often you have no choice but to melt snow for water. Melting snow may seem self-explanatory, but surprisingly enough, you can mess it up and end up with some pretty unpalatable stuff. Your first step in making decent water is to use a clean pot. Pots with bits and pieces of breakfast stuck to the sides are going to give you water with bits and pieces of breakfast in it.

Likewise, try to get clean snow. If you gather snow from under a pine tree, you will end up with lots of pine needles in your water. So if possible, get snow from the middle of a meadow where you are less likely to have things falling down from above.

Your next step is to pour some starter water into your pot. Believe it or not you can burn or scorch snow. Snow crystals form around a nucleus of dirt, which can actually burn, giving your water a terrible flavor. To avoid scorching your snow, start with an inch of water in the pot. Turn on the stove and start warming the water. Slowly add snow, stirring

Put about an inch of water into your pot before adding snow when making water. Otherwise, your water will taste burnt. ALLEN O'BANNON

as you go. Once you have a couple of inches of liquid in the bottom of the pot, you can fill the entire thing with snow and stop stirring. If you are making water to store overnight, do not bother to get it hot. That's just a waste of fuel. The water needs merely to be liquid to ensure you have fluid in the morning to start breakfast. Remember to bury your water in snow overnight to ensure it does not freeze.

If you do not have any starter water, you can avoid scorching your water by putting a small amount of snow in a pot over heat and stirring vigorously until you get some melting. It's kind of like shaking the popcorn pot. If the snow keeps moving, you are less likely to get burning.

CHAPTER 6

Winter Hazards

Going out into the outdoors has its own inherent hazards, just like getting into a car. Those hazards do not mean you shouldn't go, but they do mean you need to be knowledgeable and aware. Winter's hazards are a bit more extreme than summer's, in the same way winter driving is more extreme. Cold temperatures, snow, ice, and harsh weather are challenging and can be dangerous for the unprepared.

Cold

Cold is an inherent part of winter, and for the most part, you just deal with it. You wear more clothes, you eat more, you carry more gear, you create shelter, you do what you need to do to keep yourself warm and comfortable. But sometimes you blow it—or someone in your party blows it—and gets too cold. It's not hard to do: Maybe a piece of equipment breaks and strands you out overnight without any camping gear. Maybe someone falls through the ice and gets everything wet. Or maybe a prolonged storm pins you down. There are any number of scenarios that can result in someone getting too cold. Probably most people who've spent any time in the outdoors have experienced it at least once. I know I have.

When you stop for breaks, put on a hat and parka right away to conserve the heat you've worked hard to generate. MOLLY ABSOLON

What this means is, you can work to avoid the problem with adequate preparation, but you'll also want to know what to do if things don't go the way you plan.

Hypothermia

Hypothermia is when your core temperature drops below its comfortable 98.6°F average. As your temperature falls, you begin to lose your fine motor skills. You can't zip up your jacket, and your coordination may seem off. Gradually these signs intensify and are accompanied by changes in your ability to think rationally or make good decisions. You may also begin to shiver uncontrollably.

At NOLS we taught people to beware of the "umbles": stumbling, bumbling, mumbling, and grumbling. The key thing is that people's personalities and physical abilities deteriorate as they get colder. Ideally you want to stop the progression as quickly as possible. So if you notice you are apathetic and it takes you a while to put on extra layers even when you know you should, ask yourself if you are getting too cold. Watch your teammates for similar symptoms, and do something immediately to prevent further chilling.

With mild hypothermia you can usually stem the progression by exercising. Run around your camp, do some jumping jacks, swing your arms and legs. Make sure your clothes are dry, and get out of the wind and cold. Drink something warm, and eat some food to fuel your engine. Typically these actions will have immediate results: You'll feel better. Your coordination will return. You'll be warm.

With more moderate hypothermia, people tend to get increasingly apathetic. You may just feel like sitting down and cuddling up in a ball. You may begin to be increasingly incoherent and slow to respond to questions, and your responses to those questions may be inappropriate. As you get colder, you may lose your coordination and be unable to walk without falling. Finally, when a person becomes severely hypothermic, he or she will be unresponsive and it may be hard to detect a pulse. As people deteriorate, it becomes increasingly difficult to reverse the trend. A severely hypothermic person has to be rewarmed in a hospital.

For someone who is moderately cold, start by making sure he or she is in warm, dry clothes and out of the elements. If the individual is capable of drinking from a cup by herself, give her warm fluids and a snack. If the person shows no signs of improvement after these initial steps, you'll need to be more aggressive in your treatment. One of the most effective methods for treating moderate hypothermia is to make a hypothermia wrap (see sidebar on next page).

If your patient is severely hypothermic, gently place him in a hypothermia wrap. Take care not to be too rough in your handling of the patient, as sudden movements can cause heart problems in a severely cold human. The hypothermia wrap will not rewarm your patient, but it will help prevent further heat loss. Go for help. This individual will need medical attention, but even if he appears dead, there is hope. Often severely hypothermic people are successfully rewarmed. The saying in the first-aid world is that someone is never dead from cold until they are warm and dead.

Hypothermia Wrap

1. Lay out a large ground cloth or tarp flat on the ground.

2. Place a sleeping pad under a sleeping bag in the middle of the tarp.

3. Have your patient get into the bag wearing dry base layers and a warm hat.

4. Place hot water bottles at the patient's feet, in his groin area, and under his armpits. (Avoid placing the bottles directly against the skin to prevent burning.)

5. Snug up the sleeping bag hood around your patient's face, leaving a small hole for him to see and breathe through. Wrap the ground cloth around the sleeping bag as if you were swaddling a baby, again making sure to leave a space open for his face.

6. Keep replacing the water bottles as the patient cools. Keep him wrapped up in this cocoon until he returns to normal. Note that if your patient has been really cold, he is likely to be worn out by this ordeal and will need to rest for a day or so before resuming normal activity levels.

When someone is too cold to warm up by exercise, create a hypothermia wrap: place the individual in a sleeping bag with hot water bottles and then wrap her up in a waterproof, windproof tarp. MOLLY ABSOLON

Frostbite

Frostbite is the freezing of tissue, so it can only occur when temperatures are below freezing. Frostbite typically affects our extremities, because our bodies shunt blood away from those expendable appendages to keep our precious core and brain warm, which means less blood flow in your fingers and toes and a higher likelihood of them freezing.

Frostbite is evaluated like a burn: superficial, partial thickness, and full thickness. The thickness refers to your skin tissue, so superficial frostbite just affects the top layer of skin, while full thickness frostbite affects all the way through the skin layer into your subcutaneous fat. Full thickness frostbite can cause permanent damage and loss of tissue.

Make it a habit to check your feet routinely. Avoid wearing constricting clothing or too-tight boots to help enhance circulation. And make sure to stay hydrated.

Finally, don't tolerate cold feet or hands. If your toes or fingers get numb, stop and do something about it. You can swing your legs and arms; you can do jumping jacks. If your feet don't seem to be rewarming through exercise, ask a friend if you can put your cold body part on his or her stomach. That first touch will be rather brutal for your Good Samaritan, but it's a great way to warm up your hands or feet.

Superficial frostbite is also called frostnip. It's when you get spots of white on your cheeks or nose after a cold ride up the chairlift, for example. Usually you can rewarm superficial frostbite by simply blowing warm air on the spot. If it's on your face, cup your hands together around your face and blow. Make sure to cover up after the spots disappear, as the warming is only temporary if the conditions that caused the problem haven't changed.

Partial thickness frostbite can be difficult to distinguish from full thickness in the field. Your toes or fingers will display many of the same symptoms as full thickness, but may not be as hard. Full thickness frostbite will be unmoving to the touch, like wood. Regardless, if you are in the field and your toes or fingers appear to be frozen, you have a simple choice: to rewarm or not to rewarm?

To rewarm a frostbitten appendage, submerge the affected part into a warm water bath (temperatures between 104°F and 108°F). You must keep the water at this temperature, which means constantly replenishing the bath since your frozen body part will cool it down. Rewarming is painful, as probably most of you know if you've ever thawed out chilled toes or hands. Climbers call the pain "the screaming barfies," it's that bad. If you choose to rewarm the appendage, give your patient (or yourself) something for the pain before you begin the process. Ibuprofen helps, but something stronger would be great if you have it.

Most likely, if you are deep in the mountains in the winter, it will be difficult to warm and keep warm a frozen part. Plus, you may no longer be able to use that part after it's thawed, as you are likely to have fluid-filled blisters, swelling, and pain. So, in some situations, it may behoove you to keep the part frozen while you make your way to civilization. Repeated freezing and thawing can cause more damage than one-time freezing and thawing.

Non-freezing Cold Injuries
Immersion Foot

Non-freezing cold injuries can also happen in the winter. The most common of these is immersion foot. Typically immersion foot takes place in wet temperatures a little above freezing, so temps in the 30s and 40s are prime.

Immersion foot results in excruciating pain and nerve damage. Some of the signs you learn in first-aid class—mottled, grayish feet—don't actually show up in all cases. This means the best way to prevent immersion foot is to recognize when conditions mean it is possible, and be diligent about keeping your feet warm throughout the day.

Snow Blindness

The glare of the sun off the snow can burn your corneas. The result is pain and light sensitivity that lasts for twenty-four hours, basically meaning you are stuck in place until the injury is healed. Someone

Even on cloudy days, you need sunglasses and sunscreen because of the glare off the snow. MOLLY ABSOLON

with snow blindness can do little more than sit in the dark with damp compresses over his or her eyes until the pain subsides.

Chilblains and Sun Bumps

Chilblains are a painful inflammation of the small blood vessels in response to sudden warming. Chilbains can cause redness, itching, swelling, and blistering and usually occur on the extremities: toes, fingers, nose, etc. Typically you'll notice chilblains when you return home after spending time outside in cold temperatures. Symptoms can last a couple of weeks. To prevent chilblains, avoid constricting clothing to ensure adequate circulation and try not to expose your bare skin to extreme cold.

Some people develop small blisters or pimples on their skin after exposure to UV radiation. Sun bumps, as they are called, are common in snowy conditions with intense UV radiation and usually occur on people's faces. Sun bumps can be itchy and disfiguring, but tend to go away without treatment after a week or two. The cause of sun bumps is not well understood but appears to be some kind of reaction to UV. To prevent sun bumps, wear sunblock (zinc oxide and other physical blocks seem to work best).

Raynaud's Disease

Raynaud's is a condition that causes the small arteries that supply blood to your skin to spasm, or narrow, limiting circulation in response to cold temperatures and stress. Typically Raynaud's occurs in people's fingers or toes. The result of the vasospasm is that skin turns pale or white, then blue. Often the affected area feels numb and cold, and your sense of touch is dulled. As the spasms subside and circulation improves, the area may turn red and throb or tingle.

Treatment of Raynaud's depends on its severity. For most people, the problem is more of a nuisance than a disability. Many people know they have Raynaud's before they head out into the cold, and so have developed tricks for dealing with the problem, such as carrying chemical hand and foot warmers and taking care to stay warm and dry. If you experience an attack of Raynaud's in the field, warm the affected area gently until the spasms subside and circulation improves.

Avalanches

I went out for my first ski run of the winter a few days ago and was horrified to see a line of ten people booting their way up the center of one of the most popular ski bowls in the area. To their credit, the avalanche hazard was low, but I was still amazed to see their total disregard for good backcountry travel techniques. Not only were they breaking all the rules about good routefinding, they were also destroying the ski slope.

Take time to think about the environment before you venture out. Ask yourself if an avalanche could happen and, if so, do you have the knowledge, tools, and skills to avoid or react appropriately? If nothing else, don't look like an idiot and march up the middle of a potential avalanche slope in a group of ten.

This book is not going to give you enough knowledge to go out and assess the snowpack. My goal is to help you identify the conditions that create slides and avoid hazardous terrain. If you are eager to ski slopes steeper than 30 degrees, you should get avalanche training. The American Avalanche Institute and the American Institute for Avalanche Research and Education both offer courses for beginners up through experts. Local ski shops will often host avalanche awareness clinics. I highly recommend such training if you plan to be in the mountains in winter.

Types of Avalanches

The two types of avalanches are point-release, or loose snow, slides and slab avalanches. Point-release slides are like they sound: A single point of snow releases and starts moving downhill, picking up more snow as it moves. The shape of a point-release slide is a classic teardrop. Typically these slides, also called sluffs, occur on slopes steeper than 35 degrees and often release naturally during storm cycles. Most of these slides are relatively small, although occasionally they can entrain enough snow to cause damage. The more important hazard for backcountry travelers to consider is the slide's potential to knock you off your feet into dangerous terrain. Point-release avalanches can push climbers over cliffs or cause skiers and boarders to take life-threatening tumbles.

Slab avalanches tend to be more deadly, however. Again, the name indicates the nature of the slide. Blocks of cohesive snow—slabs—release as a unit and move downhill. Slabs can be hundreds of feet across and travel thousands of feet, or they can be a few feet across and run only a short distance. It doesn't really matter, as given the right terrain, either size can kill you. Slab avalanches typically occur on slopes between 30 and 45 degrees, with 38 degrees considered "prime time."

Slope angle is the most consistent factor in avalanche mechanics. Determining slope angle is challenging. Your best bet is to invest in an inclinometer or slope meter to get an accurate reading.

Except in extreme wet snow conditions, green light terrain—or slopes under 30 degrees—are safe. But if you have steep slopes above you, beware. The other factors in creating a snow slide are more complex and include terrain, weather, and snowpack.

Terrain

North-facing slopes tend to have weaker snowpacks, at least in the early season. This is because they receive less sun, meaning less warmth to help the snow bond. (It's more complicated than that, but for now that's enough information.) Leeward slopes—or those away from the dominant wind direction—are also more dangerous because they get loaded with extra snow by the wind. More snow means more weight on the snowpack, which means more stress—which can translate into danger. Leeward slopes also often have cornices hanging over the ridgelines. Cornices can be a booby trap for an unsuspecting traveler who ventures out onto the lip unaware only to fall through, and they can break off and trigger a slide on the wind-loaded slope below. So in general, it's wise to avoid cornices.

Slope shape can also be a factor in avalanche potential. Convex slopes tend to break easier than concave ones. You'll hear people talk about the rollover zone—or the spot where the slope bends downhill.

Some avalanche paths are obvious and can be identified by the absence of mature trees, a funnel shape, and a long runout zone. ALLEN O'BANNON

The rollover is often a fracture spot because of the mechanics of the stresses on the slope. Below the rollover the snow is pulled downhill by gravity. Whether that movement is a slow creep or a break and slide depends on the snowpack.

Finally, treed slopes can be safer for travel than open slopes. But anyone who has watched avalanche videos over the years has seen images of slides crashing through trees, so the notion that trees are always safe is risky. I've heard it put this way: If the trees are spaced widely enough apart for enjoyable skiing, they do not offer protection against a slide. That said, thickly treed slopes are unlikely to avalanche. You can use this information to help you pick your route: A trail through thick forests is likely to be safe.

Trees can also help you read the area's history. A slope covered with small trees with no uphill branches indicates past slide activity and is a red flag for backcountry travelers.

Good routefinding is critical to safe travel in avalanche country. You should look for ridges, thick trees, and low-angle slopes when choosing your route. Avoid gullies or "terrain traps" where even a small slide can pile up deeply. Know what is above you. If you cannot see because of

Wind-scoured ridges make safe routes through avalanche terrain, as long as you stay well back of any undercut cornices. JERAMIE PRINE

weather or trees, read a map. Avalanches sweeping down from above have caught many a hapless traveler unaware.

If you find yourself forced to cross potentially hazardous terrain, cross one at a time. Post spotters in islands of safety, and watch each other cross. If the slope avalanches, you can mark the last-seen spot of your companion. This can shave precious time off your search by narrowing down your options.

Weather

Most avalanches occur during or right after storms. Any storm that brings in 6 or more inches of snow (and remember wind can also move snow, so a 3-inch storm can actually be loading leeward slopes with a lot more snow if the wind is blowing) can up the avalanche hazard. After storms, look for avalanches. If you see slides, it's likely you can expect more slides to occur on slopes of similar shapes and aspects.

Also, storms that come in cold and warm up are more dangerous than ones that come in warm and cool down. Why? Warm, wet snow is heavier than cold, light powder. Light on heavy is safer than heavy on light.

There's more to weather than these few simple rules of thumb. Temperature affects the snowpack, making it stronger or weaker. Rain, ice, and sun crusts can all create layers that can strengthen or weaken the snowpack.

Snowpack

Analyzing the snowpack is the most complex part of avalanche forecasting. People go to school for advanced degrees in snow science, which means this book is not the place to learn about snow morphology or crystal dynamics.

But you should be aware that you need two things in your snowpack to create a slab avalanche: a cohesive slab of snow and a weak sliding layer. The best way to know if these two conditions exist is to pay attention to the snowpack throughout the season. Around here in November 2011 as I write this, people are already talking about a weak, faceted snowpack that could be problematic throughout the season.

This means that until that weak layer disappears, people are going to be looking for it and watching to see if it causes avalanches.

Avalanche forecasters will give you an idea of what is out there. In most mountainous regions of the country, there is an avalanche hotline or website where you can get a professional evaluation of the local snowpack. That said, these forecasts are general and do not give you a free ticket to safety.

You can also dig snow pits to help you see what's what. Again, the pit just gives you information for your specific location, but if there is a big old ice layer a foot down, you can be pretty confident that ice will be all around and could be a sliding layer if the snow above is not bonding to it well. A weak layer can also let you know it's there loudly and clearly by collapsing as you travel. The resulting *whumph* sound has been described to me as nature screaming a warning: "Danger, things are unstable out here!"

Snowpack analysis is challenging for beginners, and a book is not the place to learn about it. Take an avalanche course if you think you want to be out on slopes that can slide. Travel with more knowledgeable friends, and have them explain why and how they are making their decisions. Look for signs: Broken-off trees, old avalanches, changing temperatures, rapid snow accumulation, "whumpfing" snow, and high winds are just some of the warning signs that conditions could be deteriorating and the avalanche hazard increasing.

Safety Equipment

Travelers in avalanche terrain should be equipped with a shovel and an avalanche transceiver at

Snow pits can give you information about the layers of snow beneath the surface. MOLLY ABSOLON a minimum. A probe is also a good idea. These pieces of equipment allow you to find and dig out your partners in the event of an avalanche. Without them, you may end up simply standing by while someone you care about dies.

Carrying safety equipment is useless, however, if you don't know how to use it. I've been carrying this gear religiously for twenty years, but I realized this fall I hadn't practiced with my transceiver in a few years, so I got it out to play around. I was terribly rusty. It even took me a moment to remember how to turn the transceiver from receive to search. I figured it out, but in those wasted moments, someone could die. So know how to use your gear and practice so your skills stay current and efficient.

There are other specialized pieces of avalanche equipment such as the Avalung available on the market. These things are designed to improve your survivability if you are caught in an avalanche. Skiers, snowboarders, and mountaineers use them when they enter terrain they know can avalanche.

Ice

Frozen rivers, lakes, and streams can be dangerous if the ice is not strong enough to support your weight. Still, these features can often make for easy travel in the right conditions, so it behooves you to know a few things before venturing out onto frozen bodies of water.

Ice is amazingly strong if the layer is consistent. In general, a cross-country skier can cross ice that is only 3 inches thick safely, while a light truck needs only 11 inches of ice to support its weight. That said, ice thickness varies. Currents, water depth, wind, and snow cover can all affect the consistency and thickness of ice.

Here are a few things to consider when evaluating ice:

- The inlets and outlets of lakes often have thinner ice because of water currents. Likewise, the areas of strongest currents in rivers and streams will have the thinnest ice, so avoid the outside of bends or places where the river's gradient steepens.

Frozen lakes and rivers can make good travel paths if the ice is solid enough to support your weight. PETER ABSOLON

- Objects sticking out of the ice—rocks, stumps, etc.—can trap heat, thereby causing the ice to be thinner and weaker.

- Snow can insulate ice, keeping it from freezing thickly.

Cross ice on skis or snowshoes to disperse your weight over a larger area. Keep space between people. Tap the ice with your ski pole as you move along. A solid *thunk* indicates thicker ice, while a hollow sound can mean thinner ice.

If you do fall through the ice, don't panic. Take a minute to control your breathing and relax. Dr. Gordon Geisbrecht, director of the University of Manitoba's Laboratory for Exercise and Environmental Medicine, has done a lot of firsthand research on this topic (he's plunged into icy water enough to earn the moniker Dr. Popsicle). You can see a demonstration of him in action on *The Late Show with David Letterman* on YouTube.

Dr. Geisbrecht has an expression: One minute, ten minutes, one hour. The first minute is the time it takes for you to control your breathing. Your body goes into a kind of panic in response to the shock of the cold. During this time your best bet is to try to relax and wait until you get your breathing stabilized.

Once that minute passes, you have approximately ten minutes of functional movement. This is the time you want to try to get yourself out of the water. If you know you are crossing ice, you may choose to travel with picks hanging around your neck to provide purchase on the ice in the event you fall through. Most of us, however, do not carry such things. For us, our best bet is to extend our arms across the surface of the ice, and then kick vigorously, trying to push our bodies up onto the ice. Pull with your arms to help. Hopefully this will work, and you'll end up lying on the ice. Stay horizontal and pull yourself to thicker ice or the shore.

If you cannot get out of the water, don't lose hope. Geisbrecht has found that you can still live a long time. You have approximately an hour before you are likely to lose consciousness from hypothermia and, even then, you could be revived. So your strategy is to prevent drowning. Keep your arms extended on the ice. If you are lucky, they will freeze there, holding you in place even if you lose consciousness.

CHAPTER 7 # A Final Word

Winter is just starting in Teton Valley, Idaho, as I write this. Outside, snow is swirling around my window, and the bare aspens in the yard are shuddering in the breeze. We've been out skiing twice, but winter is still new. My body isn't quite prepared. I find myself getting cold easily, and I'm sitting now with a space heater blowing over my feet. The ice that coats parking lots worries me. My adaptations are slow to come, perhaps slower because I'm not living out there in the cold where I'd have no choice.

But even as I find myself thinking with some longing of sunshine, beaches, and heat, I have waxed my skis and pulled out my ski pack. I've looked through my gear to make sure everything is in working order. I practiced with my beacon, and I've had those two runs where I felt the joy of the speed and saw the beauty of the snow-covered trees and the sparkle of the surface hoar.

Winter in Teton Valley typically lasts well into April or May. Some even say it lasts until June, so I'd better love it. And I do, but I also recognize that taking that first step to get out there is daunting. It's daunting every year, and I've been doing this for twenty years now. So have confidence. We all have to readjust. It's well worth the effort, for winter is a magical, beautiful time to be outside.

Appendix

Repair Kit Checklist

- ❑ Duct tape

- ❑ Epoxy or barge cement

- ❑ Seam grip

- ❑ Rip-stop tape

- ❑ Sewing kit

- ❑ Zipper sliders of various sizes (check tent zippers, jackets, etc.)

- ❑ Stove replacement parts (spare pump, valve, cleaning tool, oil, etc.)

- ❑ Pliers, vise-grip, or multi-tool

- ❑ Speedy stitcher

- ❑ Spare ski binding parts

- ❑ Spare ski basket

- ❑ Ski pole splint

- ❑ Wire

- ❑ Parachute cord

- ❑ Multi-bit screwdriver

Day Pack Checklist

- ❑ Insulated jacket

- ❑ Mittens or gloves

- ❑ Goggles and sunglasses

- ❑ Hat and neck warmer

- ❑ Food

- ❑ Water

- ❑ Thermos (optional)

- ❑ Shovel

- ❑ Avalanche transceiver and probe (destination dependent)

- ❑ Small first-aid kit

- ❑ Small equipment repair kit

- ❑ Sunscreen

- ❑ Wind or Gore-Tex layer

- ❑ Maps

Index

A

alpine huts, 60–61
American Avalanche Institute, 101
American Institute for Avalanche
     Research and Education, 101
Appalachian Mountain Club, 12
Athabascan people, 68
avalanches
     courses and training, 55,
          101, 105
     point-release, 101
     probes, 51, 55, 73, 106
     safety gear, 55
     slides and slab, 101
     transceivers, 55, 105–6
     as winter hazard, 6, 7, 55,
          100–106
Avalung, 106

B

Backcountry Magazine, 21
bedtime in your shelter, 79–82
Black Diamond, 56, 57–58
Black Diamond Megamid, 57

C

camping in winter
     bathroom etiquette, 83–84
     bombproofing, 68
     campsite selection, 66
     equipment, 61–63
     getting settled down, 67–68
candle lanterns, 62
carbon monoxide poisoning, 78
catholes, 83
chemical hand and foot
     warmers, 80
classes on winter hiking and
     camping, 12
clothing. *See also* footwear
     basic winter clothing list,
          48–49
     choosing warm clothing,
          43–49
     cotton, 47
     damp clothing, 80–81
     down and pros and cons, 46
     Gore-Tex and pros and cons,
          46–47
     hats and hoods, 49
     and heat loss through
          convection, conduction,
          radiation, and evaporation,
          43–44, 45
     insulation, 44, 46
     layering, 47–49
     managing moisture, 44–45
     materials, 45–47
     mittens and gloves, 49, 81
     synthetics and pros and
          cons, 45
     wool and pros and cons, 46

zippers and zipper pulls, 49
contact lenses and contact
    solution, 63
convex slopes, 102
cornices and slopes, 102
crampons, 56
Cross Country Skier Magazine, 21

D
deadman anchors, 59
destinations, choosing, 5–7
digloos, 73–75
doghouses, 76

E
emergency shelters, 76
Ensolite, 80
excercise and heat generation,
    44, 80

F
fall line, 37, 38
flashlights and spare
    batteries, 62
food
    and alcohol, 87–88
    breakfasts, 87
    calories, 85, 87
    cheese, 87
    cooking tips, 88–89
    day food, 85–86
    frozen foods, 88
    overnight food, 86–88
    prepping food in town, 88
    and thermosses, 85–86, 87

footwear
    booties, 49, 80
    gaiters, 1, 48–49
    hiking boots, 1–3, 80
    overboots, 3, 49
    racing boots, 26
    ski boots, 26
    socks, 48, 80, 81
    winter boots and removable
        liners, 80
forests, 9

G
Geisbrecht, Gordon, 107–8
GPS, 6

H
hazards in winter
    avalanches, 6, 7, 55, 100–106
    chilblains, 99
    cold temperatures and
        inclement weather, 6,
        93–94, 104
    frostbite, 97–98
    hazardous terrain, 102–4
    hypothermia and hypothermia
        wraps, 94–96
    ice and frozen lakes and
        streams, 6–7, 106–8
    immersion foot, 98
    non-freezing cold injuries,
        98–100
    open water, 6
    Raynaud's disease, 100
    snow blindness, 98–99

snowpack hazards, 104–5
sun bumps, 99–100
hiking boots
    booties, 49, 80
    gaiters, 1, 48
    as means of winter
        transportation, 1–3
    overboots, 3
    postholing, 2, 3
hot water bottles, 80

I
ice ax, 56
ice ax ski pole, 56
inclinometer, 101

L
lanterns, 62
leeward slopes, 102
lip balm, 63

M
moling, 71–74
Mountaineers, 12
MSR Whisperlite, 61

N
Nalgene bottles, 63
National Outdoor Leadership
    School (NOLS), 12, 25, 68, 85, 94
Neos, 3

O
organization, 79

P
pee bottles, 63, 83
personal items, 63–64
Petzoldt, Paul, 68
planning your trip, 8–12
poles
    and baskets, 27
    and cross-country skiers, 27
    and downhill skiers, 27–28
    falling down and getting up,
        19, 41
    pole length, 27
    ski poles, 16–17, 26–28
    telescoping poles, 28
    trekking poles, 16–17
pots, skillets, and utensils, 62
Powder Magazine, 21

Q
qhinzees, 68–73
quarrying, 74

R
repair kits, 56–57
Restop, 83
rollover zone, 102–3

S
safety equipment, 55, 105–6
saws for snow, 54–55
seasons
    fall, 8–9
    spring, 8, 31
    summer, 10
    winter and midwinter, 8–9, 10–11

shelters, 57–61
shovels, 54
Sierra Club, 12
Ski Magazine, 21
skiing
    alpine turns, 21, 22
    breaking trail, 40
    controlled sit-down, 41
    downsides, 4–5
    falling down and getting up, 41
    flats, 32–33
    herringbone, 36
    kick turn, 18, 37, 38, 40
    kicking and gliding, 32–34
    as means of transportation, 4–5
    pole placement, 38
    sidestepping, 37
    travel techniques, 32–42
    uphill techniques, 34–37
skis
    accessories, 26–31
    alpine-touring (AT) skis, 22, 26
    backcountry touring, 23
    bindings, 22–23
    climbing skins, 28–29
    cross-country skis, 21
    glide wax, 24
    kick wax, 23, 24
    metal edges, 22
    Nordic cross-country skis, 20
    renting, 19
    single and double-camber skis,
        20, 21, 25
    skate skis, 21
    ski length, 26

ski poles, 26–28
    and skins, 28–31, 36
    snakeskins, 29
    telemark skis, 22
    and terrain, 21–22
    touring skis, 21, 23
    types, 21–26
    wax and waxless, 22, 23–25, 31
    wax for skis, 24–25, 31
sleds, 53–54
sleeping bags, 62–63, 82
sleeping systems, 62–63
slope meter, 101
snow
    basic principles, 65
    crystals and facets, 65, 91
    snow blocks, 74–75, 76
    snow caves, 73, 76
    snowpacks, 65, 102
    work-hardened, 70
snow conditions, 8–9
snow kitchens, 76–79
snow shelters, 60, 68–76
snow temperature estimate, 25
snowboards and snowboarding,
    1, 5, 15, 106
snowshoeing
    breaking trail, 18–19
    falling and getting up, 19
    kick turns, 18
    as means of winter
        transportation, 3
    side-hilling, 17
    travel techniques, 17–19
    traversing a slope, 17

walking backward, 18
walking downhill, 18
walking over flats, 17
walking uphill, 17
snowshoes
    backcountry or
        mountaineering, 15
    bindings, 14, 15
    cleats, 15
    and hiking boots, 16
    hiking snowshoes, 14
    mountaineering-style
        snowshoes, 9, 16
    pack boots, 16
    price range, 13
    recreational shoeshoes, 14
    running or racing
        snowshoes, 14
    and terrain, 9
    types, 14–15
    and your weight, 15
stoves, lighters, and pads
    fuel, 61–62, 79, 89, 90–91
    lighting stoves, 88–91
sunglasses, goggles, and
    bandanas or cloth, 64
sunscreen, 63

T

tarps, 57–58
tents, 57
terrain, 9

Therm-a-Rests, 63
toiletries, 63
trailbreakers, 40
Trailspace Backcountry Gear
    Guide, 13
travel distances and travel time,
    10–12
tree wells, 76
treed slopes, 103

W

waste products, 83–84
water
    for drinking, 51, 86
    evaluating ice, 106–7
    frozen, 106
    melting, 91–92
water bottles, 63, 80
Whippet, 56
white gas, 61–62
white gas lantern, 62
winter cuisine, 85–92
winter packs
    ease of access, 50
    hydration system, 51
    materials, 51
    pack fit and guidelines, 51–52
    size, 50
    straps, whistles, and bells, 51

Y

yurts, 60–61

About the Author

Molly Absolon is a former National Outdoor Leadership School (NOLS) instructor, an environmental educator, and outdoor writer. She is the author of the *Backpacker* Magazine Core Skills books *Campsite Cooking*, *Trailside Navigation*, *Trailside First Aid*, and *Outdoor Survival*. She lives in Teton County, Idaho, with her husband, Allen O'Bannon, and daughter, Avery.